MW00940910

Metaphysics
A guided tour for beginners

TOMASZ BIGAJ

PHILOSOPHY OF BEING, COGNITION AND VALUE
AT THE UNIVERSITY OF WARSAW

Published in the United States under the auspices of
Philosophy of Being, Cognition and Value
at the University of Warsaw

Cover photo: Ewa Bigaj

ISBN: 1475055404
ISBN-13: 978-1475055405

CONTENTS

ACKNOWLEDGMENTS

I would like to thank Ewa Bigaj, Mariusz Grygianiec, James Ladyman and Abe Witonsky for reading and commenting on earlier versions of this book.

INTRODUCTION

The term "metaphysics" elicits mixed responses. For some metaphysics is the ultimate science of reality, surpassing all other branches of knowledge in depth and beauty. But for others metaphysics has a checkered past and a somewhat tarnished reputation. To begin with, even the term itself is a result of a historical accident. When one of the greatest philosophers of all time Aristotle died in the fourth century BC, he left reams of written notes on virtually all scientific topics imaginable – from logic, politics, and ethics, to astronomy and botany. His pupils and followers took up the colossal task of organizing those manuscripts into separate works, known today collectively as the *Corpus Aristotelicum*. However, they had a considerable difficulty with categorizing a group of particularly abstract and hard to comprehend writings dealing with such issues as the notion of being and substance, the first causes (or principles) of things, the notions of one and many, the problem of change, the existence of mathematical objects and of one God. Rather than subsume these writings under any extant category, the decision was made to place them in order following the treatises on physics, and therefore the provisional title "Metaphysics" was coined, which literally means "what comes after physics". But the name stuck, and to this day is associated with the most general and abstract philosophical considerations regarding what exists. Much later another term – "ontology" – became popular as an alternative to "metaphysics". "Ontology" is a blend of two Greek words: *on* which means "being", and *logos*, interpreted in this context as "science". Some philosophers treat the terms "ontology" and "metaphysics" as synonyms, but it is also common to use the former in a narrower sense to refer to the part of metaphysics which analyses the most general categories of objects (known as ontic categories) constituting reality.

Throughout its long history metaphysics has undergone numerous transformations, both in subject and method. There were times when metaphysics had the reputation of a highly speculative branch of philosophy, disconnected from experience and common sense. Some philosophers in the 17th century attempted to build comprehensive and rather abstract metaphysical systems purported to reveal the ultimate nature of reality. For instance the Jewish-Dutch philosopher Baruch Spinoza argued in a very convoluted way that everything is made of one substance which is identical with God, whereas the German polymath Gottfried Wilhelm Leibniz insisted that the ultimate elements of the universe are independent and isolated souls called monads. But such unbridled speculations drew a lot of criticism and even contempt from a broad spectrum of philosophers. Among the most prominent critics of metaphysics were the Scottish thinker David Hume and the German philosopher Immanuel Kant. Hume believed that the only way to acquire knowledge about the external world is through the senses, and therefore it is impossible to have direct access to reality not mediated by our experience. Kant agreed with this claim and consequently with Hume's critical approach to speculative metaphysics. However, Kant vowed to restore the good name of metaphysics (in a new form referred to by him as "critical") by focusing his investigations on the fundamental concepts such as time and causality which are necessary to form any knowledge whatsoever. Such a new metaphysics should subsequently become the foundation of all scientific knowledge.

Hume's radical anti-metaphysical stance echoes in many later philosophical schools, in particular the influential 20th-century school of logical positivism. Philosophers associated with this movement argued that metaphysical claims are not only fundamentally unknowable, but even meaningless. For them any meaningful statement must meet the stringent requirement of *verifiability*; that is it must be possible to prove conclusively that it is true (in later versions of verificationism this condition was replaced by a slightly less strict requirement that for all meaningful statements it should be possible either to prove that they are true, or to prove that they are false). Logical positivists believed that science passes the verificationist test of meaningfulness with ease while metaphysics definitively fails it. Thus the only meaningful general statements about the world can be found in the fundamental scientific theories, such as physics or astronomy. However, as it turns out even legitimate scientific claims can have difficulties with satisfying the verificationist criterion if they are sufficiently universal. Nowadays the verificationist principle is considered to be thoroughly discredited, and metaphysical statements are back in favor.

The tide began to turn in favor of metaphysics in the second half of the last century. Even scientifically oriented philosophers came to the realization that scientific theories by themselves cannot offer us a unified and clear picture of reality. Different theories in science are based on different, sometimes even incompatible fundamental assumptions regarding the nature of the world, and to make matters worse some theories do not uniquely determine their proper "metaphysical" interpretations. Thus one important problem that the metaphysician can take up is trying to answer in most general terms the question of what the world should be like for a given scientific theory to be true. Another possible area of fruitful metaphysical investigations is a reconstruction of the metaphysics of common sense. What objects should be assumed to exist, and what structure should the world possess, for our basic, pre-philosophical and pre-scientific intuitive beliefs to be vindicated? If this task is accomplished, the next step may be to compare the reconstructed metaphysics of the person in the street with the metaphysics arising from accepted scientific theories. What intuitive beliefs regarding the world should we abandon as a result of scientific progress, and what beliefs can we retain? All these questions require of course a developed conceptual framework of basic metaphysical notions, such as the notions of object, existence, identity, property, temporality, persistence, causality, and many more. Thus it should not come as a surprise that modern metaphysics occupies itself extensively with the task of defining these fundamental concepts in various ways and selecting the best characterizations available.

This short book gives a brief and elementary overview of a selection of central problems discussed in contemporary analytic metaphysics. Although most of these problems are deeply rooted in classical philosophical schools and doctrines, I will present them in a modern philosophical guise, as it is commonly done on the pages of current philosophical journals and books. One conspicuous feature of this modern approach to metaphysics, which will show in this book, is its heavy reliance on other branches of knowledge, including logic, semantics, mathematics, and all areas of natural sciences with physics at the forefront. To begin with, the classical metaphysical question of the existence and identity of objects cannot be properly approached without a strong support from modern logic and semantics. The same applies to yet another traditional metaphysical debate on the nature of so-called universals. Discussions on the existence and nature of abstract entities are part and parcel of modern philosophy of mathematics, hence the connections between metaphysics and mathematics are strong in this field. Logic gives us a new insight into another famous metaphysical debate on the meaning of necessity and possibility. But it has to be admitted that the presently dominating logical analysis of these notions gives rise to a number of new, previously unknown metaphysical questions, such as the problem of the status of possible worlds. Further on we will see how modern physics influences and shapes the age-old philosophical topic of time and temporality. One particularly exciting question is whether physics implies that the experience of the passage of time which we all have is just some sort of an illusion with no deeper ontological meaning. Physics has a say in current discussions on the notion of causality as well. It turns out that the metaphysics of causation can also benefit from the logical analysis of modality, and in particular the logical semantics of counterfactual conditional statements. Finally, we will consider the fascinating question of the relation between the doctrine of determinism and the apparent existence of freely acting agents, that is us. We will witness yet again how this metaphysical question can be approached using a mixture of physics, psychology, and logic.

1 EXISTENCE AND IDENTITY

Existence is one of the most fundamental notions of metaphysics, and also one of the most resistant to explanation. As we already noted in the Introduction, a significant portion of metaphysical analysis concerns the problem of what categories of objects can be identified as constituting parts of reality. The word "reality" may be just interpreted as "all that exists". Thus metaphysicians should have a good understanding of what it means for something to exist. We will start our attempt to clarify the notion of existence by looking carefully at how this word functions in natural language. Let us begin by labeling affirmative sentences of the sort "The South Pole exists" or "Electrons exist" as positive existential statements. But sometimes we would like to deny that something exists. In that case we have to make use of negative existential statements.

Negative existential statements are typically used to indicate the fictional character of some concepts. Thus we can explain to a child that fairies don't exist, or that the famous detective Sherlock Holmes never existed. But negative existential statements also play an important role in science. For example, astronomers at the beginning of the 20th century put forward the hypothesis that there should be yet another planet in the Solar System which orbits the Sun closer than Mercury. This hypothetical planet was even given the name of Vulcan, after the Greek god of fire. However, such a planet was never detected in spite of an extensive search, hence the conclusion was drawn that Vulcan does not exist. In mathematics some negative existential statements form important theorems. An example can be Euclid's famous theorem about the nonexistence of the greatest prime number. Finally, philosophers often advance negative existential statements with respect to "suspicious" entities postulated in certain theories, such as abstract objects or mental events.

But there is a semantical problem brought about by negative existential statements. Let us consider the statement "Vulcan does not exist". What is this statement about? If, as its grammatical structure suggests, we interpret it as being about its subject, that is Vulcan, we have an immediate difficulty here. For it looks as if Vulcan had to exist in order for the sentence "Vulcan does not exist" to be true. Clearly, a statement is about something only if this something exists, otherwise it would be about nothing. But this leads to a contradiction: Vulcan both exists and does not exist. This is an age-old philosophical problem known already to the Greek philosopher Plato, and sometimes even referred to as the Platonic riddle of nonbeing. Below we will consider two possible solutions to this paradox, which will lead to two rather different conceptions of what existence is.

Non-existent objects

One way out of trouble is to divorce the notion of existence from the notion of an object. We may choose to admit that Vulcan is something – an object – but this object happens to be a non-existent one. This leads us to a metaphysical conception, according to which all objects can be divided into two groups: existent and non-existent ones. In the first category we can find familiar entities: trees, planets, cars; whereas the second category of non-existent entities is filled by all sorts of fictions: unicorns, fairies, planets closer to the Sun than Mercury, and so on. The main proponent of non-existent objects was the Austrian philosopher Alexius Meinong (and hence modern followers of his theory are often called neo-Meinongians). He believed that all concepts we can come up with must refer to something which he called objects of thought. Sometimes these objects of thought turn out to be real, that is existent, but in some other cases they remain mere figments of our imagination. But this does not rob them of the status of an entity.

The conception of existence that emerges from these considerations is often referred to as the property view. This is so, because according to this view existence is a property of some objects. Just as the property of being red differentiates objects that possess it from objects that don't, existence merely separates all entities into two groups depending on whether they are real or not. But there is an ontological notion even more general than existence which is available to the metaphysician – that is the notion of *being*. There are unicorns, but they don't exist. The proponents of the property view admit that there are objects which don't exist. Existence implies being, but being does not imply existence, the same way as being a horse implies being a mammal but not vice versa.

The property view of existence seems to be very natural and intuitive. However, the underlying conception of non-existent beings encounters serious difficulties. First of all, the domain of non-existent objects must be rather large, perhaps even outnumbering the realm of ordinary, existing entities. Each concept, no matter how outlandish, must have its counterpart at least in the domain of fictions. Consider, for instance, the description "The x-foot-high golden mountain", where x is any real number. To each such description there should correspond one non-existent object. This already implies that there is at least as many distinct fictional objects as there are real numbers. Moreover, there is the problem of contradictory objects. Is there a non-existent square circle? If yes, then some object possesses two mutually inconsistent properties of being square and not being square (e.g. being circular).

Another problem is related to the fact that non-existent objects are incomplete with respect to their properties. For instance Vulcan can be said to possess definitely only two properties: being a planet and being located within the orbit of Mercury. But other possible properties of Vulcan are fundamentally indeterminate: its mass, its diameter, period of revolution, period of rotation, the tilt of its axis, etc. are not determined, as they don't enter into the definition of the concept of Vulcan. This stands in sharp contrast to the way existent objects behave. Even though we may not know many properties of the existent planet Mercury, we have good reasons to believe that no matter what possible characteristic of a planet we choose, Mercury either possesses it or not. Because of their incompleteness, in many cases it is impossible even in principle to decide whether some non-existent objects are one and the same entity or distinct objects. Consider, for instance, the non-existent planet Vulcan whose diameter equals 16,654 miles, and the planet Vulcan whose period of

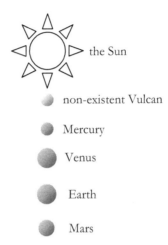

the Sun

non-existent Vulcan

Mercury

Venus

Earth

Mars

Is this what our solar system would look like if we admitted
non-existent objects?

revolution around its axis equals 73.4 hours. Are they identical or
distinct? But how could we possibly decide, if it is in principle
indeterminate what the period of revolution of a planet is, given only
its diameter? The American philosopher Willard van Orman Quine
famously quipped that there are no entities without identity. If the
matters of identity or distinctness are not settled in a given domain,
the items in this domain do not deserve to be called objects, or
entities.

It is controversial, to say the least, to assume that non-existent
objects can possess properties in the same way existent objects
possess their properties. Consider again our fictional planet Vulcan.
We are being told that this non-existent planet literally exemplifies
the property of being located somewhere between Mercury and the
Sun. But we have extensively scoured this area using our best
astronomical instruments, and we've failed to notice anything that
remotely resembles a planet in the vicinity of the Sun! How can an
object have the property of being located somewhere without actually
being there? You may point out that non-existent objects cannot be
observed. True, but we have not defined Vulcan as a non-existent
being, but as a planet. And isn't it part of what we mean by being a

planet that it has to be in principle possible to observe it? (If you are not happy with this interpretation of the concept of a planet, we can always modify our definition of Vulcan as to include the phrase "a planet which can be in principle observed".) Some modern neo-Meinongians try to get around this problem by postulating that non-existent objects do not literally possess their respective properties, but instead are only "defined" or "constituted" by them. But this desperate defense does not help much. When astronomers introduced the concept of Vulcan for the first time, they did not define it as an object which is "constituted" (whatever this may mean) by its appropriate properties, but as something that should literally possess them. And when they announced the negative result of their search, they didn't say that the object *constituted* by the properties of Vulcan does not exist, but rather that the object which literally *possesses* all its properties does not exist. For all we know it may be even true that the unique object constituted by the properties of Vulcan does exist (for instance as an abstract entity, or a mental concept). But this object is not Vulcan itself, and is of no interest to astronomers.

Finally, the property view of existence runs into deep troubles related to the way we define our concepts. As we have seen, we typically build our definitions by combining together various properties. But if existence is just one more property, what can stop us from using it in our definitions? Let us then define the concept of E-Vulcan as follows: it is an object which is a planet, which is located closer to the Sun than Mercury, and which exists. And now we have a problem similar to the one we started with. If we want to state that E-Vulcan does not exist (as there is clearly no existing planet between Mercury and the Sun), we will have to contradict ourselves by admitting that an object which possesses, among other properties, the property of existence does not exist. A similar trick has actually been used in the famous ontological proof for God's existence, formulated in the 12th century by St. Anselm of Canterbury. St. Anselm defined the notion of God using the property of being the greatest entity imaginable, and then argued that possessing this property necessarily implies existence. From the perspective of the property view St. Anselm's inference seems perfectly reasonable. The concept of God has to have its referent, whether existing or not. But if the objective counterpart of the notion "God" possesses all its definitional properties, it must also possess the property of existence, and hence God must exist. The trouble is, however, that an analogous argument can be applied to virtually every conceivable concept (for instance that of the most perfect island imaginable), and this is surely unacceptable.

The quantifier view of existence

There is an alternative solution to the paradox of non-existence. It is based on the assumption that negative existential statements, such as "Vulcan does not exist", are not about their grammatical subjects at all. The German philosopher, logician and mathematician Gottlob Frege has suggested that existential statements are actually about concepts and not objects. When we say that Vulcan does not exist, what we really mean is that the concept of Vulcan does not refer to anything (that it is empty). And according to Frege concepts are perfectly acceptable entities whose existence is not questioned. However, Frege's interpretation of existential statements is not the only one available. Yet another approach is associated with the names of two famous logicians: Bertrand Russell and Willard V.O. Quine.

It may be observed that when we state that Vulcan does not exist, we are in fact talking not about the non-existent Vulcan, but in a way about all objects in our universe. We simply want to say that there is no Vulcan among them, or more precisely, that no object in our universe possesses all the properties attributed to Vulcan. This in turn translates into the statement that no object in the universe is a planet closer to the Sun than Mercury, or even simpler, that no planet is closer to the Sun than Mercury. Clearly, the last statement does not require for its truth that there be any non-existent object. But one consequence of this approach is that existential statements are not what they seem to be. An existential statement has to be reformulated in order to reveal its genuine logical structure, different from its grammatical form. In spite of their superficial similarity, the sentences "Vulcan does not exist" and "John does not smoke" have different structures. Only the latter sentence is truly about one individual – John – to whom the property of being a non-smoker is attributed. The former statement however makes a general claim about a whole class of objects (e.g. planets). Such statements are called in logic "statements of quantification".

Let us consider another example of an existential statement, for instance "Electrons exist". Again, we have to stress that this sentence is not about electrons, but rather, in a special way, about the entire universe (or domain, as it is called in logic). It namely states that among all things in our domain at least one object can be found which has the property of being an electron. In logic such a statement is often presented semi-formally as follows: "There is an x such that x is an electron". The symbol x is called a variable, and its role is to represent any unspecified object in the domain. The phrase "There is" in turn is known as a quantifier, or more specifically the existential quantifier. Thus it can be said that the word "exist" reduces to a quantifier. Returning to our example of a negative existential statement "Vulcan does not exist", it can be translated into the following, slightly cumbersome expression: "For all x, x is not a planet closer to the Sun than Mercury". The expression "For all" is yet another quantifier, called the universal one. Its meaning should be clear – we are using it when we want to talk about everything at all with no exception.

The logic of the quantifier conception of existence may be slightly daunting, but the underlying metaphysical picture is really simple. There is no division of beings into the categories of existent and non-existent objects. The broadest domain of being contains only existent objects. Everything that exists is an object, but it is also true that each object exists. The word "exists" is equivalent to "there is", "is an object", "is an entity", etc. Consequently, no fictions can inhabit our domain. If they are included in the domain, they are not fictions any more. Existence is not a property which could be denied to some objects. If we still insisted to refer to existence as a property, we would have to accept that it is a universal one, namely such that all objects possess it. In short, according to the presented conception everything exists.

The last consequence is often criticized as highly unintuitive. After all, we are accustomed to the view that not everything exists: unicorns, elves and little green men don't exist. But we have to remember what the scope of the word "everything" is in the current approach. By everything we mean every object in our domain, and there are no non-existent objects in the domain. A downside is that now we cannot literally say that there are some things which don't exist (such as fictions). Perhaps the best way to express the intuition behind this thought is to say that not all concepts refer to something (there are concepts which are empty).

The quantifier view of existence, in contrast to the alternative property view, stresses logical connections between the term "existence" and other expressions of natural language. Suppose for instance that someone utters the statement "Some thoughts of philosopher A are difficult to understand". On the surface this expression does not make any existential claim, as it does not contain the term "exist". However, under closer scrutiny it may be revealed that the above statement has certain existential implications. To see this, we may want to translate the initial utterance into the logical form "There is an x such that x is a thought of philosopher A and x is difficult to understand". And now we may observe that in order for this statement to be true, our domain must contain at least one object satisfying the entire formula following the "such that" expression. In short, our domain must contain at least one thought of philosopher A which is hard to understand. This commits us to the acceptance of the ontological thesis that thoughts exist.

The reasoning we have just presented illustrates the essence of what is known as Quine's criterion of ontological commitment. Quine claims that the way we build our statements determines what sorts of entities we should accept into our ontology. In order to reveal the ontological commitments of a given sentence (or a whole theory) we have to follow a two-step procedure. First, the sentence has to be translated into standard logical language (known as the first-order language). Then, it has to be determined what objects should belong to the domain of the theory in order for this translated sentence to be true. Quine notes that certain words in natural language, such as pronouns "something", "nothing", "anything", carry important ontological implications. We should typically translate them into quantifiers and variables, and those in turn are directly related to what exists, as we explained earlier. If in the end we are not happy with the commitment to a certain category of entities that have been revealed as a result of the procedure, we can always try to reformulate our original expressions. This is known as the method of paraphrase, and is extensively used in various ontological debates, as will be seen later in the book.

It has to be admitted, though, that the method of paraphrase is not unanimously accepted as a proper tool in philosophy. Some philosophers point out that it is fundamentally flawed, because the proposed paraphrase is either logically equivalent to the original statement or it is not. If the first is the case, then the paraphrase will have exactly the same existential consequences (two logically equivalent statements have exactly the same logical consequences). But in the second case it may be claimed that the paraphrase is inadequate. To this we may reply that the paraphrase need not be logically equivalent with the original statement: all we really need is that it expresses roughly the same thought.

Numerical identity and qualitative identity

Identity is another fundamental notion of metaphysics without which it would be virtually impossible to follow modern discussions on the subject. To begin with, two interpretations of the notion of identity have to be distinguished. When we say that two snowflakes are identical, what we roughly mean is that they look so similar that they can't be told apart. This notion of identity is known as qualitative identity, and is usually explicated as possessing the same properties. Sometimes qualitative identity is also referred to as indiscernibility. But there is another, more basic interpretation of identity. In this fundamental sense, when we say that object a is identical with object b, we want to express the thought that a and b are one and the same object – that there is not two but one individual bearing two different labels "a" and "b". The relation between a and b in this case is called numerical identity, and is usually symbolized with the help of the equality sign: $a = b$.

At first sight numerical identity seems to be relatively unproblematic. I am numerically identical with myself and nothing else, and similarly this chair is numerically identical only with itself. However, it is rather difficult if not plainly impossible to properly express these intuitions in the form of a direct definition. If we tried to define the relation of numerical identity as holding between each object and itself, and nothing else, such a definition would be circular, because the term "nothing else" already presupposes numerical distinctness (when I say that I am not identical to anything else than me, this can only mean that I am not identical to anything that is not identical to me). The best we can manage is to characterize generally the analyzed relation in an abstract sort of way by citing its main formal properties. Numerical identity clearly possesses the following properties: (1) it holds between each object x and itself (this property is called reflexivity), (2) if it holds between object x and object y, it also holds between y and x (this is called symmetry), and (3) if it holds between x and y and also between y and z, then it holds between x and z (this is called transitivity). But unfortunately there are many relations which satisfy all these three conditions. It can be easily checked that the relation of being born on the same day is reflexive, symmetric and transitive, and yet I am not numerically identical with all people that were born on the same day that I was. Relations satisfying all three conditions (1)-(3) are called equivalence relations. Clearly numerical identity is an equivalence relation, but there are equivalence relations other than identity.

However, an interesting fact can be noted. It turns out that the relation of numerical identity is in some sense included in all equivalence relations. This is an immediate consequence of the fact that all equivalence relations are reflexive. If R is an equivalence relation (for instance being born on the same day), and an object a happens to be numerically identical with object b, then clearly a stands in relation R to b (obviously I was born on the same day that I was born on). This fact can give us a hint of how to finally define what numerical identity is: it is namely the smallest equivalence relation possible in the sense of being included in all equivalence relations. This may not look like a particularly illuminating definition, but it's better than nothing.

Numerical identity gives philosophers even more headaches. Gottlob Frege has struggled with a seemingly simple and naive question: how can an identity statement be true and at the same time informative? Suppose that I have stated that object a is numerically identical with object b. There are two possibilities now: either a is in fact an object distinct from b, or they are indeed numerically identical. If the first is the case, then my claim is false. On the other hand the claim I have made is true only when a and b are just one and the same object. But it is trivial to assert that an object is identical with itself – everybody knows that. Hence if what I have said is true, it is trivial and uninteresting. But how can this be the case, given that there are plenty of examples of identity statements which advance our understanding of the world? Ancient Babylonian stargazers had every right to be surprised and amazed when they realized that one bright star visible in the night sky just after the sunset (and hence appropriately called the Evening Star) is the same object as another star observed before dawn (the Morning Star). Frege solved the problem by distinguishing two important roles played by individual names. A name picks out one particular object (called its reference), but it also carries certain meaning (its sense). It is possible that two names with different senses can nevertheless point toward one and the same object. And it is possible to use two names having different senses without knowing that they refer to the same object. Thus a discovery that $a = b$, where names "a" and "b" have different senses, does not have to be trivial or insignificant.

Now we have to ask important questions about the relation between numerical identity and qualitative identity (indiscernibility). Does numerical identity imply qualitative identity, and vice versa? The answer to the first question is usually given in the form of so-called Leibniz's law, or the Principle of the Indiscernibility of Identicals. This principle states that if a is the same object as b, then a and b possess exactly the same properties. Clearly if the Morning Star is numerically identical with the Evening Star, and the Morning Star has the property of being the second planet from the Sun, then the Evening Star ought to be the second planet from the Sun as well. Leibniz's law is considered to be a law of logic, and thus necessarily true. It is easy to notice that when $a = b$, if a had a property P which b did not possess, one and the same object would have P and not have it at the same time, and this is impossible.

The only conceivable threat to Leibniz's law can come from taking into consideration so-called intensional contexts. The hero of the famous sci-fi story, Superman, is the same person as Clark Kent, but Lois Lane does not know that. Consequently, she is in love with Superman, but not with the unassuming journalist Clark Kent. Thus it looks like we have a counterexample to Leibniz's law, for it is true that Superman has the property of being loved by Lois Lane whereas Clark Kent does not have this property in spite of being the same person. One way of repelling this counterexample is to admit that attributes which involve somebody's beliefs about an object (known as intensional attributes) do not constitute acceptable properties of this object. Other types of intensional expressions include so-called modal notions which will be discussed later in this book.

The Principle of the Identity of Indiscernibles

More interesting from the metaphysical point of view is the principle known as the Identity of Indiscernibles (PII for short). It states that if object a is indiscernible from object b, then a and b are numerically identical. Another way to express this thought is by saying that two numerically distinct objects are always discerned by their properties (this can be called the dissimilarity of the distinct). It is important to notice that the meaning and status of the PII depends on how broadly we interpret the term "property" in the definition of indiscernibility. Suppose we accept that each object has a certain property of being this particular object. For instance this chair can be said to possess the property of being identical with this very chair and nothing else. If we agree to use such properties in order to discern objects, then it trivially follows that numerically distinct entities are always discernible, and thus PII is true. For if a is a distinct object from b, a possesses the property of being a, and b possesses the property of being b, which in this case are clearly different properties. But most philosophers agree that properties such as being this particular thing should not be included among the qualities which can discern objects. We should distinguish between so-called pure (or qualitative) and impure (non-qualitative) properties. Impure properties involve reference to particular objects, times or places (an example: being the eldest son of Napoleon), whereas qualitative (pure) properties don't (the property of being the eldest son of a general who has won more than five battles is pure). It is commonly accepted that the notion of discernibility should be analyzed in terms of pure properties only. Thus two objects are discernible if there is a pure, qualitative property which is possessed by one but not by the other.

There are further distinctions to be made within the category of qualitative properties. It is customary to distinguish between intrinsic (non-relational) and extrinsic (relational) properties. A relational property is a property possessed by an object a with respect to a different object b. For instance, being a husband is a relational property, because one can't be a husband without being married to someone else. But the property of being a six-foot-tall person is (presumably) intrinsic, as it does not depend on the existence of anything other than the person who is six feet tall. Now we can introduce two notions of discernibility – discernibility with respect to intrinsic properties only, and discernibility with respect to intrinsic or extrinsic properties. Consequently, we arrive at two variants of the Principle of the Identity of Indiscernibles. The strong version of PII states that two distinct objects have to be discernible with respect to their intrinsic properties. The weak version, on the other hand, claims that distinct objects should be discerned by their intrinsic or extrinsic properties. Thus two exactly identical metal spheres made of pure iron and having precisely the same dimensions would violate the strong but not necessarily the weak PII, because they could still be discerned for instance by being located in different parts of the universe.

The German philosopher Gottfried Leibniz believed that the strong version of PII is necessarily true. For him the spheres described above are not only hypothetical, but impossible. However, Leibniz failed to provide a satisfactory proof of his claim. Nowadays philosophers generally believe that a formal proof of PII can't be given, however there may still be arguments showing that PII is worth having. The Principle has a strong appeal for empiricists, because its denial implies that there may be an ontological difference without any difference in observable qualities. The defenders of the PII point out that without it we couldn't for instance refute the seemingly absurd claim that there are one hundred and ten indistinguishable desks in front of me instead of just one. Assuming PII is true, we can reduce facts about numerical identity and distinctness to facts involving qualitative properties only. For instance we could say that to be numerically distinct from object a is just to have a property that a doesn't possess.

However, all these advantages of the PII cannot change the fact that it is in serious danger of being conclusively refuted. To begin with, the above-mentioned example shows that the strong version of PII is not a necessary truth, meaning that it could be false. Max Black, a British-American philosopher, modified the example so that it can be applied to the weak version too. Suppose that the universe contains nothing else except two identical iron spheres 2 miles apart. In such a universe the spheres are not discernible even by their relational properties, since there is no third object which could stand in some relations to one of them and not the other. Thus even if the weak PII is true in our world (which is obviously not like Black's world), it is only contingently true, which means that it could very well turn out to be false. And recent developments in physics give us reasons to believe that PII may be actually violated in our world. Individual elementary particles of the same type, such as electrons, protons, and photons, do not differ from each other with respect to such basic properties as mass or charge. In classical physics particles can still be discerned by their different trajectories, as long as we accept that they are impenetrable. But in quantum mechanics particles are not assumed to have definite trajectories. Instead, they are characterized by wave functions which may "spread" in space and overlap with one another. Even worse for PII, in the quantum theory of many particles the so-called indistinguishability postulate is introduced, which states that an exchange of particles of the same type should not have any observable, or measurable effects. This postulate leads to a restriction of available states which particles of the same type can jointly occupy, and this in turn proves that individual particles of the same type should be ascribed exactly the same relational and non-relational properties.

The way quantum theory describes states of many particles of the same type is notoriously difficult to visualize, but we may try to make it slightly more intuitive by considering the following example. Suppose we have two electrons whose wave functions are well separated in space from each other. We may be tempted to ascribe to each electron different spatiotemporal properties related to "its" wave function, but we have to take into account the fact that the state of the entire system of two particles should remain the same when we swap both electrons (in the case of electrons their joint state has the formal property of being "antisymmetric", meaning that swapping the electrons results only in the change of sign in the entire formula describing the state). This implies that the state of one individual electron is actually not given by a separate wave function, but in a sense by a probabilistic combination of both functions (this is technically called a "mixture"). The state occupied by both electrons is known as "entangled", and of each separate electron we can only say that it has a fifty-fifty chance of being found in the location of one wave function, and a fifty-fifty chance of being found in the location of the other wave function. Because this can be said of both electrons, it follows that they are actually not discerned by their properties. Thus PII seems to be violated.

One way of saving the Principle is to modify further the notion of discernibility on which it is built. A suggestion has been made by Simon Saunders, an Oxford philosopher of physics, that a different grade of discernibility, known as weak discernibility and introduced earlier by Quine in a different context, should be applied to quantum particles. Two objects a and b are said to be weakly discernible if there is a relation which holds between a and b but not between a and itself. Thus Max Black's spheres are weakly discernible by the relation "being 2 miles from", since one sphere is 2 miles from the other one, but clearly not from itself. It turns out that quantum elementary particles known as fermions (electrons and protons, but not photons, are fermions) can be weakly discerned as well. But it remains controversial whether the Principle of the Identity of Indiscernibles based on weak discernibility is even related to the PII as conceived by Leibniz. Suffice it to say that weak discernibility clearly does not enable us to tell two objects apart. It can only ensure that there are two objects rather than one. Thus it can be maintained that the relation of weak discernibility can play the role of a qualitative ground for numerical identity and distinctness, but its introduction does not advance other empirically-motivated claims associated with the traditional PII.

2 UNIVERSALS AND PARTICULARS

The distinction between universals and particulars is almost as old as philosophy itself, as it can be traced back to the great Ancient thinkers – Socrates, Plato, and Aristotle. The concept of universals derives directly from the observation that individual things display striking similarities which enable us to categorize them into general kinds. Classification of objects and processes is the beginning of all science, as without it we wouldn't be able to discover and describe any regularities. Most probably even the language that we speak would not be possible without us recording similarities between things. A natural metaphysical explanation of the fact that things of a given kind (trees, chairs, electrons) have something in common is to assume the existence of an extra object which stands in a particular relation to those things. For example, a red rose and a red car can be said to resemble each other because of a third object, redness, that is somehow present in both objects.

In that way we have introduced a new type of objects – universal objects, or universals for short. Universals are supposed to be related to ordinary things in a special way. This relation is known as instantiation, or exemplification. A red rose and a red car both exemplify one universal: redness. Objects which can only exemplify, but are never exemplified themselves, are now referred to as particulars. But some universals can exemplify other universals as well. For instance redness, which is a universal, exemplifies the property of being a warm color. Thus we can have a whole hierarchy of objects ordered with respect to the relation of instantiation. At the bottom of the hierarchy are particulars, then universals exemplified by particulars (so-called first-order universals), then universals exemplified by the universals from the previous level (second-order universals), and so on. We can also make another important distinction between monadic and polyadic universals. Monadic universals are primarily properties, although some insist to include in this category a separate type of universals known as kinds. Properties are called monadic (from the Greek word *monos* – alone, single) because they can be instantiated by individual, single objects. Polyadic universals (the Greek word *polys* means "much"), on the other hand, are relations. Relations are exemplified not by single individuals, but by their pairs (in the case of dyadic universals) or triples, quadruples, etc. To illustrate, the relation of being the father of is exemplified by the pair (David, Solomon).

Postulating the existence of universals can help us analyze the semantic structure of basic sentences of natural language. Let us consider the subject-predicate statement "Socrates is courageous". It is natural to interpret this sentence as being true when the individual named by its subject "Socrates" possesses (exemplifies) the property represented by the predicate "is courageous". More precisely, two semantical functions of linguistic expressions are usually distinguished: that of denotation and connotation. An expression denotes a thing if it can be truthfully said about this thing. The name "Socrates" denotes one individual, namely Socrates himself. On the other hand, the predicate "is courageous" denotes all individuals of whom it is true that they are indeed courageous. Thus predicates typically denote more than one individual object. But each predicate also picks out a single object which is a universal. The predicate "is courageous" naturally singles out the property of being courageous. However this predicate cannot be said to denote courage. Clearly it is not appropriate to say that courage is courageous. Hence we need to introduce the new semantical function of connotation. The predicate "is courageous" denotes courageous individuals, but connotes the property of being courageous. It is usually assumed that individual names, such as "Socrates", do not connote anything. We don't use such names to pick out any property of an individual, but rather to pick out the individual as a whole.

A similar analysis can be applied to sentences involving relations (polyadic universals). The statement "Socrates is the teacher of Plato" is true if the relation "being the teacher of" is instantiated by the pair (Socrates, Plato). According to this analysis (which at this point slightly departs from the standard grammatical approach) the entire sentence can be broken down into three components: two individual names "Socrates" and "Plato", and one two-argument predicate "is the teacher of". The individual names denote appropriate people and connote nothing, whereas the predicate denotes all pairs of individuals such that the first one is the teacher of the second one. Besides that, this predicate connotes the binary relation "being the teacher of", which is a polyadic universal.

The assumption of the existence of universals can also account for the phenomenon of abstract reference in natural language. Abstract reference occurs when we use a noun which cannot be literally interpreted as referring to any particular. Examples of abstract reference are numerous. It is present in the following sentences: "Redness is a color", "Courage is a moral virtue", "These two statues have the same shape", "All objects share at least one property". The terms "redness", "color", "courage", "moral virtue", "shape" and "property" can be interpreted as names of appropriate universals. To appreciate how commonplace the phenomenon of abstract reference is, the reader is invited to randomly select a few sentences from this book and see for herself how many names referring to universals they contain

Realism and nominalism

The metaphysical position according to which universals exist is known as conceptual realism, or realism for short. Realism can come in various forms depending on how broad in scope the category of universals is assumed to be. Unrestricted realism, also known as semantic realism, asserts that to every meaningful predicate of natural language there corresponds a universal. Thus there is the property of being red, because we have the predicate "is red", and there is the property of being round connoted by the predicate "is round". But on top of that there is also a separate universal "redness and roundness" which corresponds to the predicate "is red and round". Therefore it should be clear that unrestricted realism must postulate a vast number of distinct and yet mutually connected universals. Some critics point out that this proliferation of universals is unnecessary, and in special cases it can even lead to serious logical problems.

David Armstrong, a contemporary Australian philosopher, for instance, argues against the existence of disjunctive properties, i.e. properties built with the help of the connective "or". Let us consider as an example the predicate "has mass m or electric charge q". It is unconvincing that each object which possesses mass m, and each object which possesses charge q, should in addition instantiate an extra universal "mass m or charge q". Intuitively, we would not say that a thing with mass m and another thing with charge q are in virtue of these properties similar to each other. Armstrong also points out that there are no interesting facts or generalizations which would involve such a strange "mass/charge" property. Moreover, disjunctive properties possessed by a given object can be easily multiplied by simply adding any property P whatsoever to a property actually possessed by the object. Thus we would have to admit that a rose not only exemplifies redness, but also redness or blackness, redness or courage, redness or madness, and so on.

A more abstract argument can be supplied showing that unrestricted realism actually leads to contradiction. To see this, let us consider the predicate "is not exemplified by itself". This is clearly a meaningful predicate, as it can be applied for instance to the property of being courageous (surely a property cannot be courageous). On the other hand, some properties are indeed exemplified by themselves, for instance the property of being a universal. So unrestricted realism demands that there be a property corresponding to this predicate, that is the property of not being exemplified by itself. Let us symbolize this property by X, and let us ask the question whether it exemplifies itself or not. If X exemplifies itself – that is if property X possesses property X – then from the description of what property X is it follows that X does not exemplify itself. But if X does not exemplify itself, then we can say about X that it possesses the property "not being exemplified by itself", and hence it exemplifies itself. This shows that no matter which option we choose, we end up accepting two contradictory statements. This argument is a variant of the famous Russell paradox which was originally formulated for sets, not properties. In our context it shows that there can't be a property corresponding to every meaningful predicate.

There is yet another paradox associated with unrestricted realism which is worth mentioning here due to its historical connections. We have already presented the realist's preferred analysis of sentences of the sort "Socrates is courageous". According to this analysis, the statement is true if Socrates exemplifies the property of being courageous. But it may be observed that the statement "Socrates exemplifies courage" is in need of a similar analysis. As it seems, this new statement is true if the relation of exemplification is exemplified by the pair (Socrates, courage). This time we are left with a sentence involving three objects: exemplification, Socrates, and courage. And yet again this sentence is true if the higher-level relation of exemplification is exemplified by this very triple. Clearly, this procedure can be repeated indefinitely, if only we assume that to each predicate "is exemplified by" there corresponds a separate polyadic universal. Thus the analysis proposed by the unrestricted realist lands us in an infinite regress. This regress has some similarities to the well-known third man argument used by Aristotle against Plato's conception of universals. The original argument goes as follows: if there is a universal corresponding to all men (the property of "manhood", or better "humankind"), then there should be another universal corresponding to all men plus the first universal, and yet another universal corresponding to all men together with the two previously introduced universals, and so on ad infinitum.

Historically, the Platonic and Aristotelian versions of realism are differentiated by their separate accounts of the nature of universals and their relation to particulars. Plato insisted that universals exist independently of particulars in a special realm of being known as the world of ideas, which is different from the physical and spatio-temporal world we inhabit. But according to Aristotle universals exist only insofar as there are particulars which exemplify them. Aristotle claimed that universals exist "in" things rather than "before" them. Today we distinguish two types of realism. Radical realism states that there are universals which are not exemplified by any particulars, for instance the property of being a unicorn. Moderate realism, on the other hand, assumes that only exemplified universals exist. There is no property corresponding to the predicate "is a unicorn", but the notion of a unicorn can be explained in terms of two exemplified universals: being shaped like a horse, and having a single horn.

It remains open, though, where to draw the line separating the predicates which connote real universals from the predicates which don't. Armstrong for instance subscribes to a very restrictive version of realism, which not only assumes that there are no unexemplified universals, but also rejects the existence of common-sense universals such as being human or being a tree. Armstrong believes that the only existing universals are those which are used in our most fundamental scientific theories, in particular physics. An example of a genuine universal can be the property of having the electric charge of the electron. If we adopt the physicalist view, we may argue that all high-level properties that we commonly use in everyday life can be ultimately reduced to combinations of most fundamental physical properties.

The metaphysical position which opposes conceptual realism is known as nominalism. The word "nominalism" comes from the Latin term *nomen* meaning "name". The early proponents of this view insisted that there are no universals, only universal names, hence the term. Nominalists criticize realists for multiplying entities beyond necessity. The problem with universals is not only that they are too many, but also that they are troublesome entities. According to radical realism of the Platonic sort, universals are not spatiotemporal, so they can't be observed or interacted with. How, then, can we gain any knowledge of them? On the other hand, Aristotelians can agree that universals occupy space and time, since they are "in" things. But this causes new problems. How can one and the same object be located in different places at the same time? Take for instance the color red, which is instantiated by two objects: a red rose and a red tulip. This implies that the property of being red is multilocated: it is completely and entirely present both where the rose is and where the tulip is. Multilocation defies our basic intuitions. It is certainly peculiar to admit that an object can be located 2 meters from itself (if the rose and the tulip happen to be 2 meters apart, the color red exemplified by the flowers is located 2 meters from itself).

Another problem related to universals is how to answer questions about their numerical identity and distinctness. So far we have been associating universals with linguistic entities (predicates). But is there a one-to-one correspondence between predicates and universals? Suppose we take two distinct predicates. Does their distinctness imply that the universals corresponding to them will also be distinct? It seems that the answer to this question should be in the negative. Although the predicates "is a car" and "is an automobile" are distinct, they presumably pick out one and the same property. In the light of this example it may be suggested that two predicates which are satisfied by exactly the same objects (we call such predicates co-extensional) always represent the same property. But this does not seem to be correct. Consider the following two predicates "has a heart" and "has kidneys". As it happens, all animals which possess a heart are also equipped with kidneys, and vice versa. But we don't want to admit that the property of having a heart and the property of having kidneys are identical. Clearly we could imagine a living and fully functioning creature with a heart but without kidneys. One proposal of how to solve the problem of identification of properties will be analyzed later in the book when we will have some modal notions at our disposal.

The most radical version of nominalism, austere nominalism, insists that there are only particular, concrete objects, such as people, trees, electrons. Austere nominalists do not believe that we have to postulate universals in order to analyze semantical features of natural language. The function of denotation is all we need to describe the truth conditions for simple sentences. The statement "Socrates is courageous" is true if the object denoted by the name "Socrates" is among the objects jointly denoted by the predicate "is courageous". No mention of the property of being courageous is necessary here. The biggest problem for the austere nominalist is posed by the phenomenon of abstract reference that we discussed earlier. Let us consider for instance the statement "Triangularity is a shape". As it stands, this statement presupposes the existence of universals through the use of two abstract nouns "triangularity" and "shape". The nominalist who wants to express the thought encapsulated in this sentence without endangering his metaphysical views must resort to the method of paraphrase. This method consists in replacing the original statement with a substitute which best expresses the required meaning but does not make illicit reference to anything that is not a particular. In our example the following replacement may be suggested: "All triangular objects are shaped objects". This statement is free from abstract reference, as it clearly speaks about concrete objects only. But austere nominalists cannot offer a unified, principled way of paraphrasing away each and every statement which contains abstract reference. Troublesome statements have to be dealt with on a case-by-case basis, and there is no guarantee that a required paraphrase will be found. Consider for instance the sentence "Courage is a moral virtue". It would be incorrect to translate it by analogy with the previous case into the statement "All courageous people are morally virtuous", for the latter is undoubtedly false (there are for instance courageous criminals). Another difficult example could be the statement "This tulip and that rose have the same color". Clearly, paraphrasing it as "This tulip is red and that rose is red" is inappropriate, since the original sentence does not mention any specific color, only that it is shared by both flowers.

Some nominalists realize that they need to postulate more entities than austere nominalism would allow in order to ensure that their method of paraphrase will work. Metalinguistic nominalists include linguistic expressions among their accepted entities. That way they can replace terms referring to putative universals with terms describing linguistic expressions (predicates). Thus the truth condition for the statement "Socrates is courageous" can be expressed with the help of the relation of satisfaction between objects and linguistic expressions: the statement is true if Socrates satisfies the predicate "is courageous". The sentence "Triangularity is a shape" is explicated as "The expression 'is triangular' is a shape predicate", and "Courage is a moral virtue" gets translated into "The expression 'is courageous' is a virtue predicate". The statement about the tulip and the rose can be taken care of in an analogous manner: "This tulip and that rose satisfy the same color predicate". However, some problems remain. Consider for instance the statement "All pairs of objects have at least one property in common". It expresses a different thought than the nominalistically acceptable version "All pairs of objects jointly satisfy at least one predicate", since it is quite reasonable to expect that we don't have in our language predicates corresponding to every existing property, so the first sentence may be true in spite of the second being false. Moreover, it is not clear what the ontological status of linguistic expressions is, and whether the nominalist can accept them with no qualms. Expressions understood as individual inscriptions or utterances (so-called tokens) should not prick the nominalist's sensitive conscience. But when we talk for instance about the predicate "is courageous", we don't mean this particular inscription but rather an entire category (type). And types of linguistic expressions look dangerously similar to universals.

One key motive for introducing universals was to explain the ubiquitous phenomenon of similarity between individual objects. Metalinguistic nominalism does not seem to offer a good explanation of why we see certain predicates as more natural than the others. Why does natural language contain the predicate "is red" but does not have a predicate which would be satisfied by the planet Venus, the Tower of London, and my left thumb? The answer offered by resemblance nominalism is that red things are more similar to one another than the three random objects listed above are. Resemblance nominalism tries to develop and apply the notion of objective similarity between particulars without recourse to universals. The idea is to use the notion of similarity to define groups of objects which we commonly associate with properties: red objects, spherical objects, humans, etc. One possible strategy to achieve this goal may be as follows. We can define so-called resemblance classes by postulating that objects within a resemblance class are more similar to each other than they are to anything from outside the class. Of course we need also add the requirement that resemblance classes should be maximal (i.e. they should be the largest groups possible satisfying the requirement of similarity), otherwise we would have to admit that each single object defines its own resemblance class (each object is more similar to itself than to anything else).

Unfortunately the above definition of resemblance classes won't work. It can be easily verified that common properties do not form resemblance classes in the defined sense. Take redness as an example. It is perfectly possible to find a non-red thing which is more similar to a given red object than this red object is to another red object. For instance, two cubes of precisely the same dimension, mass, etc., one being red and one yellow, seem to be more similar than the red cube is to a two times bigger red sphere. The major problem for resemblance nominalism is that it can only use a coarse-grained "averaged" notion of overall similarity, whereas what we really need is similarity with respect to a particular quality. If we could, for example, use the notion of being similar with respect to color, the definition of redness would not be problematic. We could just point at any red object and say that redness is what is common to all objects which are most similar to this object with respect to color. But those respects seem to be none other than our old universals, hence they are not available to the nominalist.

One interesting solution to this stalemate is offered by the so-called trope theory. It postulates a new kind of entities – tropes – which may be acceptable to moderate nominalists. Tropes are individual properties: the redness of this rose, the height of that tree. Two numerically distinct particulars can never share a trope. The redness of this particular rose is distinct from the redness of that tulip. Thus tropes do not suffer from the problem of multi-location or multi-instantiation. But their main strength lies in the possibility of defining a relation of similarity between tropes which does not require any aspects. We may safely say that two tropes of redness are always more similar to each other than they are to any other trope. There is no need to specify the respect in which we are supposed to compare two tropes of redness, since the aspect is already included in the fact that they are tropes of redness. Thanks to that we can finally define a category corresponding to the property of redness as the set of all tropes which are similar to one another more than to anything else, and which contain a particular trope of redness.

It may be instructive to consider the question of the validity of the Principle of the Identity of Indiscernibles (PII) in the theory of tropes. At first sight it looks like PII becomes trivially true when applied to tropes instead of properties. Two numerically distinct individuals can never share all of their tropes, since tropes belonging to distinct individuals are always distinct. Thus it may be observed that trope theory supports the strongest version of PII imaginable, according to which sharing even one trope makes the individuals *a* and *b* numerically identical. But there is an alternative way of interpreting PII which leaves its truth open to debate, as it should be. We may define the relation of indiscernibility as follows: two particular objects *a* and *b* are indiscernible, if each trope of *a* is similar to a trope of *b*, and each trope of *b* is similar to a trope of *a*. The indiscernibility of individuals defined in such a way does not trivially imply that they are one and the same individual. But the final twist of the story of the PII in trope theory comes from considering the discernibility of tropes themselves. Because the numerical distinctness of tropes follows from the numerical distinctness of their bearers, it seems that there may be two intrinsically indiscernible and yet numerically distinct tropes (example: the trope of redness of this rose, and the trope of redness of that tulip). Hence the strong PII is violated by tropes.

Abstract objects

There is another important ontological category which is closely related to that of universals. The category of abstract objects (or abstracta, for short) is typically assumed to be wider in scope than the category of universals. There is no general consensus as to how to define abstract objects; however we can give a list of broad characteristics that are usually attributed to them. First and foremost, abstract objects are assumed to exist outside space and time. The term "outside" should not be interpreted literally in the spatiotemporal sense, but rather as indicating that it simply doesn't make sense to apply spatial and temporal properties to abstract objects. For instance, under the Platonic interpretation of universals it is inappropriate to ask where the property of redness is being located now. One consequence of the lack of spatiotemporal features of abstracta is that they cannot undergo genuine changes. This in turn implies that it is impossible for abstract objects to participate in causal interactions. As we will learn later in the book, causality is usually assumed to presuppose temporality. Non-spatiotemporal abstracta are thus causally inert – they can neither cause, nor be caused by anything. But it should be stressed that causal inertness does not imply being non-spatiotemporal. For instance, the mass centre of the Milky Way Galaxy has a precise location, and yet is not a physical object which could interact causally with other things. It is open to debate whether to include such objects among abstracta based on their causal inertness, or to exclude them based on their spatiotemporality.

One obvious consequence of the causal inertia of abstract objects is their unobservability, at least as long as we assume that any form of observation – direct or indirect – involve some kind of causal interaction. Yet another characteristic of abstracta that some insist upon is their purported ontological dependence on concrete things. According to the Aristotelian version of realism, abstract objects are derived (or abstracted away) from concrete ones. For instance, the abstract object "direction" is arrived at by considering concrete lines which are parallel to each other. The direction of a given line is what this line has in common with all lines parallel to it. But without concrete lines to begin with we could not even think about "directions in themselves". However, the derivative, dependent character of abstract objects is questioned by some metaphysicians. Platonists obviously deny that abstracta "owe" their existence to concrete things. For them abstract objects exist independently as entities in their own right.

Universals such as properties and relations form an important class of abstract objects. But there are other types of abstracta as well. We all say that linguistic expressions have meanings. Some take this literally as implying that to each meaningful expression there corresponds an object which constitutes its meaning. We have already seen that in the case of predicates there is a corresponding object, namely a universal. The meaning of the predicate "is courageous" can be thus identified with the property of courage. But what about other types of expressions, for instance sentences? What is the meaning of the sentence "Socrates is courageous"? Some philosophers insist that the meaning of a grammatically correct sentence is an abstract object called "proposition". Propositions are not linguistic entities – they exist independently of whether anybody has ever uttered of written a corresponding sentence. Two different sentences can nevertheless express the same proposition, for instance "Tom is older than Steve" and "Steve is younger than Tom". According to this approach propositions are not spatiotemporal entities, even though they may relate to spatiotemporal facts and things. The proposition expressed in the sentence "World War Two started on September 1st 1939 in Poland" is not located somewhere on the Polish-German border on that fateful day. Another related type of abstract objects is logical values. We know that the above-given sentence is true. Some philosophers believe that this implies that the considered sentence possesses the logical value of truth. Of course the other logical value would be falsity. If truth and falsity are objects at all, they clearly must be abstract ones.

Unquestionably one of the key categories of abstracta consists of mathematical objects. Philosophers have always had a keen interest in those fascinating entities. Are numbers, functions, and geometrical figures real, and if yes, what are they? How can we have any knowledge of them, and why is this knowledge so essential to our investigations of the physical world? We will only be able to scratch the surface of these important questions in this brief survey. Let us start by writing down a very simple argument in favor of the existence of mathematical entities, based on just two seemingly obvious premises.

(1) Mathematical theorems imply that mathematical objects exist,
(2) Mathematical theorems are true,
Therefore
(3) Mathematical objects exist.

The first premise may be supported by reference to Quine's criterion of ontological commitment that we discussed in the previous chapter. If we say for instance that between each two rational numbers there is a third one (this is a true mathematical statement), we therefore commit ourselves to the existence of rational numbers in virtue of the use of the existential quantifier "there is". The nominalist who wishes to challenge the conclusion (3) may want to question premise (1) by resorting again to the method of paraphrase. One possible way to do that is to try to interpret mathematical theorems as if they were statements about concrete objects. As an example let us consider a simple arithmetic truth, such as 2 + 3 = 5. It may be claimed that this statement does not actually involve abstract numbers but only concrete objects. We may interpret it as reading that if there are two objects of the kind A, and three objects of the kind B, and no object can be both A and B, then there are exactly five objects of the kind A or B. It is crucial to realize that statements of the sort "There are exactly (at most, at least) n objects of kind A" can be expressed in a language that does not refer to any number whatsoever. For instance, the sentence "There are exactly two apples in the basket" can be expressed in first-order language as follows: "There is an x and a y such that x is not numerically identical with y, and x is an apple in the basket, and y is an apple in the basket, and for all z, if z is an apple in the basket, then z is identical with x or y". This reformulation is admittedly more awkward than the original sentence but does not contain any reference to the number 2.

Unfortunately the considered method of paraphrase has a very limited scope of applicability. The vast majority of mathematical theorems cannot be treated in such a simple way. An alternative, more flexible method of explication has been proposed in order to deal with the problem of mathematical objects. For a given mathematical theorem S, it is suggested that S should be replaced with the following conditional statement: "If mathematical objects exist, then S". The last sentence does not imply the existence of mathematical entities that S speaks about, for now we are not asserting S unconditionally, but only on the presupposition that mathematical objects exist at all. And although nominalists reject this presupposition, they can still accept that if mathematical objects existed, 2+3 would be equal to 5, and there would be a third rational number between any two rational numbers. However, there is a serious problem with this solution. According to the standard logical analysis, a conditional statement of the form "If P, then Q" is always true when P (known as the antecedent) is false, regardless of whether Q (called the consequent) is true or false. This means that for the

32

nominalist all mathematical sentences become automatically true due to the falsity of their antecedent (i.e. the statement "Mathematical objects exist"). Consequently, the nominalist would have to admit for instance that the statement "If mathematical objects exist, 2+3 = 23" is true. It is possible to alleviate this problem by using a stronger type of conditional known as the strict conditional. Strict conditionals involve the modal notion of necessity, of which we will be saying more in the next chapter. But even this solution is not without serious flaws, which unfortunately cannot be discussed here due to their highly technical character.

A different strategy available to the nominalist is to deny premise (2). Arrogant as this may seem, some philosophers dare to insinuate that mathematical theorems are in fact false, the same way as fictional stories about Sherlock Holmes are. Not surprisingly, this controversial position in the philosophy of mathematics is known as fictionalism. But of course all falsehoods are not equal in mathematics as interpreted by fictionalists. Strictly speaking, both the statements 2+3 = 5 and 2+3 = 23 are false, but the first one should be accepted within the story known as arithmetic, whereas the second should not. (The same distinction can be illustrated with the sentences "Sherlock Holmes was a great detective" and "Sherlock Holmes built a time machine" – both are literally false, since there has never been a Sherlock Holmes, but only the former is part of the story written by Arthur Conan Doyle.) The main challenge faced by fictionalists is how to account for successful applications of mathematics outside its main domain of fictions. If mathematics is literally false, how can we explain the fact that bridges constructed with the help of mathematical calculations don't collapse, airplanes don't fall from the sky, and planets keep following their mathematically predicted orbits? On the basis of such observations, defenders of realism in philosophy of mathematics wheel out an argument known as the Indispensability Argument. In short, the argument points out that mathematical theorems constitute an indispensable part of our best scientific theories, and therefore receive indirect empirical confirmation from the confirmation of those theories. For instance, if precise astronomical observations confirm the general theory of relativity in physics, they also confirm the truth of the mathematical theorems used in this theory. Thus empirical evidence tells us that our mathematical theories are most probably true.

Fictionalists try to deal with the challenge posed by the Indispensability Argument by questioning its central premise that mathematical theories are indeed indispensable in science. Hartry Field, a contemporary American philosopher, has developed a strategy which could be applied to some scientific theories in order to eliminate their unwanted reference to abstract mathematical objects. Field's method is unfortunately too technical to be presented here in detail, but we can give its rough outline. The first step consists in finding, for a given mathematically formulated scientific theory T, two theories T_m and T_n such that T_n contains only nominalistically acceptable notions, whereas T_m is a pure mathematical theory, and such that the sum of T_m and T_n is logically equivalent with T. Finding such a partitioning into pure mathematical and pure nominalistic components is not an easy task, but in some cases it can be accomplished. Once this has been done, we can appeal to the logical property of pure mathematical theories known as conservativeness. Conservativeness means that when we combine a pure mathematical theory with a physical theory in order to derive a conclusion expressed in a non-mathematical vocabulary, this conclusion must also logically follow from the physical theory alone. In other words, mathematics can serve as a tool which can help us reveal logical consequences of our nominalistically-acceptable theories, but it doesn't have to be accepted as literally true. The main problem with this strategy is that we don't know how to separate many advanced physical theories, such as quantum mechanics, quantum field theory, or general relativity, into mathematical and non-mathematical components.

Sets and numbers

Mathematical objects come in various shapes and forms, as diverse as mathematical theories are. But philosophers have always been particularly interested in one category of mathematical objects: sets. Sets are considered by many as fundamental mathematical entities, because they appear in virtually all mathematical contexts, and it can be even claimed that other mathematical objects can be reduced to them (soon we will see one example of such a reduction). But it turns out that the notion of a set is not unambiguous. There are two basic ways of interpreting what sets are, and only one of them leads to the notion which proves itself useful in the foundational analyses of mathematics, whereas the other interpretation tends to be used more often by metaphysicians in their discussions of spatiotemporal, physical objects. In both conceptions sets are entities composed by some other objects, which are called their elements, or members. Let us consider as an example three apples in a basket. According to one approach, the set of those apples is just a physical object, whose parts the apples are; namely a bunch of apples. Sets interpreted as physical collections of objects are known as collective, or mereological sets (from the Greek word *meros* – part). The alternative interpretation leads to the distributive (or set-theoretical) conception of sets. We will talk about this interpretation after discussing the first one.

Mereological sets have the following characteristic features. The set containing just one object (for instance one apple) is identical with this very object. There is no mereological set devoid of any elements (you can't have a collection made of nothing). If you build two mereological sets out of numerically different objects, the resulting sets can nevertheless happen to be identical. For example, the set of three apples and the set of all atoms composing those apples are identical, even though no apple is an atom. From these characteristics it should be clear that the relation of membership in mereological sets is identical with the relation of parthood. Because of that, the relation of being an element in the mereological sense is transitive: if x is an element (part of) y, and y is an element (part of) z, x is an element of z. For instance, if my finger is part of my hand, and my hand is part of my body, then clearly my finger is part of my body.

Distributive sets differ significantly from mereological ones. They are closer to linguistic concepts than to physical collections of things. The distributive set whose member is only one object (so-called singleton) is always numerically distinct from this object – the same way as the concept of the capital city of France is a different entity from Paris itself. A set with no elements exists (and is referred to as the empty set), because it makes sense to speak about empty concepts. The only difference here is that while there are many empty concepts (the concept of a unicorn, the concept of a fairy, etc.) it can be proved that there is only one empty set. This follows from the fact that distributive sets satisfy the principle of extensionality: two sets are identical if and only if they have exactly the same elements. As a consequence, the distributive set of three apples and the distributive set of all atoms included in the apples are different sets. In fact, they have not a single element in common, since no atom is an apple. Finally, the relation of being a member is not transitive in the case of distributive sets. If you take an object x which is a member of a set y, and y in turn happens to be a member of yet another set z, the element x does not have to be an element of z (it may or may not be). Due to this fact distributive sets form an infinite hierarchy, which starts with non-sets, sets of these objects, sets of sets of these objects and so on. It is no coincidence that this hierarchy resembles the hierarchy of universals which we talked about at the beginning of this chapter. Distributive sets and monadic universals (properties) display striking formal similarities, and this fact can convince us that the former are most probably abstract objects as well.

Mereological sets, on the other hand, are not particularly troubling for the nominalist. In most cases they are just ordinary, spatiotemporal and physical things. The only controversial issue surrounding collective sets is the question whether it is acceptable to postulate the existence of collections of widely separated and disconnected objects. Is there a unique physical object made of Napoleon's left ear, the planet Jupiter, and one brick from the Great Wall of China? This problem is known as the question of composition, and some philosophers, such as the American metaphysician Peter van Inwagen, claim that objects do not always compose bigger wholes. Some further conditions need to be met for such a whole to come into being, such as spatiotemporal contiguity, or functional unity of the entire system. We will return to this question in Chapter 4 when we consider in greater detail the issue of how things persist in time.

One characteristic feature of distributive sets makes them ideal for the foundational job in mathematics, even though the very same feature can be claimed to be deeply suspicious from a philosophical standpoint. It is namely the fact that there is an abundance of sets whose existence is totally independent of the existence of non-sets, whether abstract or concrete ones. We already mentioned one such set: the empty set, which does not need any elements for its existence. But once we include the empty set into our domain, we can use it to create an infinite number of new sets. To see how this can be done, let us introduce some basic symbols. Let the sign $\emptyset$ symbolizes our unique empty set, and let us use curly brackets to indicate a set of all elements listed inside the brackets. Thus $\{\emptyset\}$ will stand for the one-element set whose only element is the empty set. It has to be stressed again that this object is numerically different from $\varnothing$ itself, therefore now we have two objects in our domain. But using these two objects we can create more and more sets, for instance $\{\varnothing, \{\varnothing\}\}$, and $\{\varnothing, \{\varnothing, \{\varnothing\}\}\}$, and so on. The sets created in this way are called pure, because they all arise out of one empty set which doesn't presuppose any non-sets.

What use can be made of such sets? It turns out that virtually all known mathematical objects can be reduced to pure sets. Let us use natural numbers as an example. As everyone knows, natural numbers form an infinite sequence: 0, 1, 2, 3, ... Such a sequence can be easily reproduced using pure sets only. We can, for instance, adopt the following identifications:

$0 = \varnothing$
$1 = \{\varnothing\}$
$2 = \{\varnothing, \{\varnothing\}\}$
$3 = \{\varnothing, \{\varnothing\}, \{\varnothing, \{\varnothing\}\}\}$
etc.

It should be easy to observe that each element in the sequence is defined as the set of all elements that precede it. Hence 0 is identified with the null-element empty set, 1 with the one-element set containing the empty set, 2 is a two-element set, and so on. It is possible to define basic arithmetic operations of addition and multiplication using only sets of the above kind. Thus the entire arithmetic of natural numbers can be reinterpreted as part of the set theory. However, a philosophical problem immediately arises. Are we supposed to interpret the above equalities as numerical identities? Is number 2 really identical with the two-element set $\{\varnothing, \{\varnothing\}\}$, the same way as the Morning Star is identical with the Evening Star? This is problematic, because natural numbers can be defined in many alternative ways, for instance as follows

$0 = \varnothing$
$1 = \{\varnothing\}$
$2 = \{\{\varnothing\}\}$
$3 = \{\{\{\varnothing\}\}\}$
etc.

In this approach all numbers starting from 1 are identified with one-element sets of increasing levels of abstraction. But the number 2 can't be identical with both $\{\varnothing, \{\varnothing\}\}$ and $\{\{\varnothing\}\}$. It looks like we have here a problem similar to the one affecting non-existent objects: the lack of clear guidelines for identity and distinctness. Some philosophers derive from this a far-reaching metaphysical conclusion that so-called mathematical objects, such as numbers, are not entities at all. According to this approach, the subject-matter of mathematical theories are not individual objects but rather their collections known as structures. It doesn't make sense to ask what the number 1 is independently from the place it occupies among other numbers. The number 1 is not an object, but a place in the structure consisting of all numbers. This claim can be strengthened by the observation that numbers lack intrinsic properties, in contrast with ordinary objects. All properties which the number 1 possesses – that it is the second number in the succession, that it is an odd number, that it is smaller than 10 – are relational properties involving other numbers. Structures are complex entities consisting of "nodes" and relations connecting them. Structures can be reduced to, or embedded in other structures. As the above examples show, the structure of natural numbers is embeddable in many different ways in the broader structure of sets. But this does not imply any statement regarding the

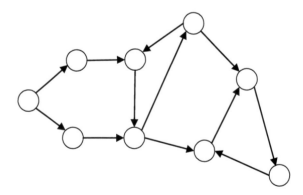

According to structuralism mathematical objects are just places in webs of mutual relations with no intrinsic properties or identity.

identification of individual numbers, because they are not independent entities but simply places in appropriate structures.

Reductive theories of particulars

So far we have focused our attention almost exclusively on universals and other abstract objects. But now the time has come to say something about the complementary category of particular, concrete objects. Nominalists believe that particulars form the most fundamental category of beings, and universals or other abstracta can be allowed into our language only insofar as they are shown to be reducible to particulars. Realists, on the other hand, have the option of treating both categories of universals and particulars as being ontologically independent. However, a third view is possible here, according to which universals are actually more fundamental, whereas particulars are ontologically reducible to universals. In this section we will analyze some reductive views on the nature of particular objects. The first reductive conception of particulars that we are going to discuss derives its motivation from empiricism. According to empiricism, we acquire knowledge about particulars through contact with their perceptible qualities. This simple observation led some philosophers, most famously George Berkeley, to believe that particular objects themselves are nothing but combinations of perceived qualities. Berkeley's original conception had the unfortunate consequence of undermining the very intelligibility of unperceived objects. But we may correct this problem by assuming that particulars are just nothing more than bundles of properties, regardless of whether they are perceived or not. This is the essence of the so-called bundle theory of particulars. According to the bundle theorist, this chair is just a collection of all its properties: weight, color, shape, the kind of material it's made from, etc. There is nothing in the chair that literally possesses its properties (there is no "bearer" of the properties).

If particulars are to be successfully reduced to sets of properties, we have to be able to distinguish groups of properties which constitute particular objects from groups that don't. For instance, the set containing, among other properties, the properties of being a horse and being winged does not identify any particular, because there are no winged horses. A typical way of dealing with this problem is to introduce the notion of co-instantiation (compresence, collocation). Normally we would say that two properties are co-instantiated if they both are instantiated by one particular object. But in the current context we can't do that, because we haven't yet defined what a particular object is (supposedly it is a group of co-instantiated properties, so we would have circularity here). Hence we will assume that co-instantiation is a primitive concept. To avoid some technical difficulties, we will also have to accept that the relation of co-instantiation can admit an unspecified number of arguments (that is, objects connected by this relation), because clearly more than two co-instantiated properties are needed in order to create a particular. (This problem can't be avoided by assuming that a particular-defining bundle must consist of properties co-instantiated pairwise, for it is still possible that different properties may be co-instantiated by numerically distinct particulars.) But it is still not enough to stipulate that particulars are to be identified with bundles of co-instantiated properties. The set containing only three properties of being cubical, being green, and being made of wood does not identify any unique particular, since there is more than one wooden green cube. We may want to add an extra condition of completeness to our bundle definition of particulars. It is not easy to define precisely when a group of properties is complete, but one approach may be to say that for every property P either P or its negation has to be included in the group. Thus, according to the proposed interpretation of the bundle theory, particulars are identified with complete sets of co-instantiated properties.

As it turns out, several objections can be raised against such a theory of individual, particular objects. One objection is that on this view all true statements attributing properties to individuals become trivially true (we call such trivial truths "analytic" or "tautologous"). Consider, for instance, the sentence "This table is wooden". If we identify the table with a set of properties, this set will contain, among others, the property of being wooden. And, presumably, the considered sentence is true if the property it attributes to the particular object is indeed included in the bundle defining this object. But it is certainly tautologous and uninformative to say that a set containing the property of being wooden contains the property of being wooden. One may suggest a way of circumventing this difficulty by reinterpreting the original sentence "This table is wooden" as the statement "The property of being wooden is compresent with the properties X, Y, Z, ...", where the symbols X, Y,

Z stand for all the properties of the table except being wooden. The fact that a given property is compresent with some other properties is clearly contingent (it may be false). But this solution lands us in even bigger trouble. Under the proposed interpretation all true subject-predicate statements about the table become logically equivalent, due to the obvious fact that the relation of compresence is symmetric. Thus saying that property *A* is compresent with *B*, *C* and *D* is the same as saying that *B* is compresent with *A*, *C* and *D*. But this means that the true statements "This table is brown" and "This table is wooden" actually say one and the same thing: that all properties of this table, including being wooden and being brown, are jointly compresent.

Another difficulty for the bundle theory comes from the problem of change. It is natural to accept that things undergo changes in time by acquiring new properties and losing old ones without losing their numerical identity. But two bundles containing different properties are numerically distinct objects. Consequently, we would have to admit that each qualitative change of a particular object is associated with the loss of its numerical identity. Perhaps one strategy of dealing with this problem is to extend the bundle definition of particulars as to include in the bundle not only the properties possessed at a given moment, but all properties that the given particular possesses even once throughout its existence. Of course in order to avoid the problem of inconsistent properties we would have to relativize properties to a given moment of time. We will talk more about this issue in one of the later chapters concerning the metaphysical analysis of time.

Finally, the bundle theory is criticized for implying the necessary truth of the Principle of the Identity of Indiscernibles. If two bundles contain exactly the same properties, they are one and the same bundle. Thus on this theory it is impossible to have two numerically distinct particulars which would be entirely indiscernible. But we should remember from our discussion in the previous chapter that PII is arguably not a necessary principle, and that there are even strong empirical arguments that it is false in our world. If we agree that PII is indeed refuted by our best scientific theories, it looks like the bundle theory will have to share PII's fate.

To avoid problems that beset the bundle theory, an extra addition to it may be contemplated. It is sometimes suggested that apart from its properties, each particular object is also constituted by an entity called the substratum. The substratum of an object is the literal bearer of all its properties, but in itself the substratum is not characterized by any properties at all (and for that reason it's often called bare substratum). The only facts that can be stated with respect to the bare substratum of a given object are facts about numerical distinctness and identity. Thus it can be said that the substratum of this chair is numerically distinct from the substratum of that table, but no qualitative difference between the two substrata can be present. The substratum theory of particulars solves the problem related to the status of PII, because it is possible now to have two distinct bundles containing exactly the same properties but numerically distinct substrata. Apparently the remaining two difficulties are also avoidable now. It may be claimed that the numerical identity of an object is retained over time in spite of changes in its properties, due to the fact that the object still possesses the same substratum. And if we agree that the subject of the sentence "This table is wooden" is not the entire bundle but only the substratum, the trivialization problem is solved, because the connection between the bare substratum of the table and the quality of being wooden is clearly contingent (not necessary).

The main weakness of the substratum theory lies in the notion of the substratum itself. John Locke, a 17th century English philosopher, famously said that the substratum is "something we know not what". For the empiricist the idea of an object with no qualitative features is deeply offensive. Moreover, it may be even argued that the concept of bare substratum is inconsistent. On the one hand, it is by definition an entity which possesses no property. But on the other hand there are nevertheless certain qualities that we attribute to substrata. We may for instance say that the substratum of this chair has the property of just that: being the substratum of this and this thing. Perhaps even the fact that substrata don't possess properties can be taken as their property (and thus the logical contradiction within the concept is clearly visible). Generally speaking, by postulating the existence of bare substrata we lose some of the advantages of an empirically-friendly reduction of particulars to universals. It may be even claimed that the substratum theory is not a reductive theory anymore, since it does not succeed in reducing completely particulars to universals. Bare substrata are objects which look more like particulars than universals, hence we have to agree

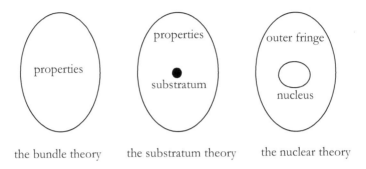

the bundle theory   the substratum theory   the nuclear theory

Three reductive conceptions of particulars

that there are "particular-like" objects not reducible to anything more fundamental.

An interesting proposal of how to reconcile the substratum theory with the bundle theory has been recently put forward by Peter Simons in his nuclear theory (for the clarity of exposition I'll ignore the fact that Simons' original theory was formulated in terms of tropes, not properties). The idea is to replace the property-free substratum with a certain subclass of properties, dubbed the nucleus. The entire bundle of properties constituting a given object is thus divided into the nucleus and the outer fringe. As long as the nucleus remains unchanged, the object retains its numerical identity in spite of superficial changes in its outer fringe. The nucleus is the proper subject of all statements about the object, and this implies that all attributions of properties included in the nucleus are necessarily true (thus the properties included in the nucleus are called essential). But the attributions of the properties from the outer fringe remain contingent, as they should be. The nuclear theory, as it seems, suffers from the same problem related to the status of the PII as the bundle theory. The only logical possibility of having two indiscernible but numerically distinct objects would be if two objects with exactly the same properties possessed different nuclei. Even more troublesome for the nuclear theory is the possibility of existence of numerically distinct objects with the same nuclei. It is natural to assume that two electrons have the same essential properties constituting their nuclei (their mass, electric charge, spin), and yet they are numerically distinct. What, then, grounds the fact of their numerical distinctness? It has to be admitted that the version of the nuclear theory which is stated in terms of tropes excludes the existence of distinct objects with identical nuclei, for numerically distinct objects always have numerically distinct tropes. However, in the context of the reductive approach to particulars the question remains what grounds the numerical distinctness of tropes of the same kind. What makes one trope of the mass of an electron distinct from the mass trope of another electron, if we are not allowed to rely on the more fundamental distinctness of the two electrons?

3 POSSIBILITY AND NECESSITY

In this chapter we will study the so-called modal notions, of which the two notions of possibility and necessity are particularly prominent. As is often the case, the term "possibility" may convey various rather disparate ideas. One of its typical interpretations can be identified as epistemic. When I say in an uncertain voice that it is possibly raining in London now, what I roughly mean is that I don't have sufficient reasons to form a strong belief about what the weather is like in London (perhaps with a slight hint that I consider rain to be more likely than not). Anyway, this use of the term "possible" points primarily to the state of my knowledge rather than to reality itself, hence the label "epistemic". Another use of the word "possible" involves a temporal perspective. This temporal perspective is present in the context of talking about future alternative scenarios. Pointing at Rodin's famous sculpture The Thinker one can say that it can be possibly painted yellow. As of now it is open whether it will be painted yellow or any other color, or left as it is. But there is a third optional reading of possibility, which can be seen for instance in the supposition that the Thinker might have been an altogether different statue, for instance another famous sculpture by Rodin The Kiss. Possibility understood as in this example is sometimes dubbed "counterfactual", although this term is a misnomer, for not all possibilities are contrary to facts in this approach. But we want to emphasize that under the counterfactual interpretation a past situation may be possible even though it actually

Could this sculpture...   ...have been shaped into that?

hasn't taken place, so in a way has been already excluded from the real world. We don't need to resort to the openness of the future to speak about possibilities in this sense. In what follows we will focus almost entirely on the third interpretation of possibility.

Modal notions and modal contexts

In modern philosophical language the notions of possibility and necessity are presented and analyzed in terms of so-called possible worlds. The question of what possible worlds are will be extensively scrutinized in subsequent sections, as it is a metaphysical problem par excellence. For now we can simply imagine possible worlds as collections of situations, or states of affairs. Situations, on the other hand, are just objective counterparts of meaningful statements. To illustrate that, the statement "This lizard is green" represents the situation that this particular lizard is indeed green (in short the lizard's greenness). The actual world can be seen as a collection of all situations which correspond to true sentences. Possible worlds also comprise of situations, but not necessarily situations that obtain in our world. But a statement describing some situation which exists in a given possible world is always true in this particular world. Thus the notion of truth becomes relativized to a world. We may also add that possible worlds are collections of situations which are in a sense complete. That is to say, for each meaningful, unambiguous sentence it should be determined whether it is true or false in any possible world. To use the words of the influential 20th century philosopher David Lewis, possible worlds are ways things might have been. If you think that the current President of the US might be a woman, you have to accept that there is a possible world in which the current President of the US is a woman.

Philosophers and logicians usually do not place any specific restrictions on the notion of possible worlds, except that they have to be logically consistent. But they admit that some possible worlds can be so far-fetched as to be epistemically "inaccessible" from our actual world. For that reason we will only focus on the worlds which are, in a suitable sense, accessible to us. Having the notion of an accessible possible world at our disposal, we can now proceed to define some important modal concepts. To begin with, we will say that a statement is possibly true (in short, is possible) if there is a possible, accessible world in which it is true. The complementary notion of necessity is defined as follows: a statement is necessary if it is true in all possible worlds accessible from our world. We may observe that any statement which is true in our world is also possible, since the actual world is just one of the possible and clearly accessible worlds. For the very same reason it is also the case that if a statement is necessarily true, it is true in our world. But there may be possible sentences which are false in our world, for instance the statement that the current President of the US is a woman. We may also introduce the category of contingently true sentences. A sentence is contingently true if it is true in our world but there is a possible world in which it is false. It can be verified that the concepts of possibility, necessity and contingency are not independent from each other. Rather, they are mutually definable. For instance, it may be stipulated that a statement is necessary if its negation is not possible. A statement is contingently true if it is true and is not necessary. Examples of necessary statements are usually taken from logic or mathematics. It is hardly questionable that the statement "It is raining or it is not raining now" must be true in all possible worlds.

The notions of necessity, possibility and contingency can be applied not only to sentences but to objects as well. An object is possible if it exists in at least one possible world, is necessary if it exists in all possible worlds accessible to us, and is contingent if it exists in the actual world but doesn't exist in some other possible worlds. Realists typically assume that abstract objects (universals, mathematical entities) are necessary, although the concept of a contingent abstract object is treated by some as a viable alternative. Some philosophers also insist that God is a necessary being (we have discussed the ontological argument for the necessary existence of God in Chapter 1). Within the framework of possible worlds we may in addition consider the notion of possible but not actual objects (merely possible entities). This concept superficially resembles the notion of non-existent entities that we criticized in Chapter 1. For instance, it may be claimed that the planet Vulcan is such a possible object, since arguably there is a possible universe in which a planet orbits the Sun closer than Mercury. But we should observe that merely possible objects avoid the main problems associated with the conception of non-existent objects. In each possible world objects are complete with respect to their qualities, and they literally possess all their qualities (Vulcan is literally located between Mercury and the Sun, since in an appropriate possible world there is a planet closer to the Sun than Mercury). In all considerations related to possible worlds the underlying conception of existence is the one expressed by the quantifier view, not the property view. The only novelty now is that we may introduce two notions of existence: actual existence, where the scope of the existential quantifier is limited to the actual world, and possible, "unrestricted" existence, with the quantifier ranging over all possible worlds.

Because of this bifurcation of existence, when we apply modal notions of necessity and possibility to statements involving quantification, things get a bit complicated. It turns out that there is usually more than one interpretation of such modal statements, and each interpretation may lead to slightly different conditions under which a given statement is deemed true. In logic it is customary to distinguish between two types of modal attributions: *de re* ("to a thing") and *de dicto* ("to a statement"). This distinction can be best explained using some examples. Consider, for instance, the false statement "There is a woman who is the president of USA in 2011". What can we have in mind when we say that this statement is possible? One interpretation may be as follows: this statement is considered possible if there is a woman in our actual world (for instance Hillary Clinton) who, although not the actual president of the US, is the president in another possible world. This explication is based on the *de re* interpretation of modality. The *de dicto* interpretation, on the other hand, states only that in some possible world the president of the US is a woman, but this woman need not exist in our world. In the *de dicto* interpretation the notion of possibility is applied to the entire statement "Some woman is the president of USA in 2011", whereas in the *de re* usage the possibility operator acts "under" the quantifier ("There is a woman such that it is possible for her to be the president of the US in 2011").

Another example of the distinction in question involves the notion of necessity. The sentence to be considered is "The number of planets in the solar system is divisible by 2", which is true in our world, given that Pluto is no longer considered a planet. But is this statement also necessary? Again, we have two options here. One is to interpret the resulting pronouncement as "There is an x which is the number of planets in our solar system, and this x is necessarily (i.e. in all possible worlds) divisible by 2". Under this, *de re* interpretation, the statement is most probably true, as it is commonly accepted that numbers possess their properties necessarily. But an alternative, *de dicto* interpretation is that for any possible world, the number of planets of the solar system in this world is divisible by 2. This is clearly a false statement, as it is perfectly possible that there may be 7 or 9 planets in our solar system.

One concept related to the above distinctions is that of a rigid designator. Let us focus on the description used in our last example: "the number of planets in the solar system". Corresponding to the *de re* and *de dicto* applications of modality considered in the last paragraph there are two interpretations of the term. In the *de dicto* reading of the modal context the term serves as a description picking out in any possible world an object which satisfies it in that world. Thus in one possible world the referent of this term may be the number 8, and in another it may be 13. But under the *de re* interpretation we took the term as referring in every possible world to one and the same object – namely the number of planets in *our* world, that is 8. Terms which pick in any possible world the same object are called rigid designators. Later in this chapter we will analyze an important claim about the way rigid designators function in natural language.

The conceptual framework of possible worlds allows us to introduce a host of other important metaphysical notions of a broadly modal character. Let us consider just one example which can be useful in various areas of metaphysics: the notions of essential and accidental properties. The essential properties of an object are typically understood as the properties without which the object could not be itself. In other words, they are necessary for it to retain its identity. For instance, I could not be myself without being a person. On the other hand, there are many properties which I could lose without endangering my self-identity, such as the property of knowing how to play piano. Such properties are known as accidental. The distinction between accidental and essential properties can be spelled out as follows. A property possessed by a given object x is essential if x has this property in all possible worlds in which it exists. Accidental properties are all the remaining properties, from which it follows that for each accidental property there is at least one possible world in which x does not have it. These definitions seem to presuppose that we have an independent criterion of numerical identity "across" possible worlds. In other words, we should be able to decide which object (if any) in a given possible world is identical with the actual object in question before we can determine its essential and accidental properties. But there is a different option here. We can namely stipulate in advance which properties we consider essential for a given object, and this decision in turn can help us decide which objects in alternative possible worlds are identical with the initial object.

What are possible worlds?

Now we will have to address the controversial question of the ontological status and nature of possible worlds. What types of entities are they? Do they exist objectively and independently, or are they reducible to some more fundamental beings? Perhaps they are just useful fictions, the same way as mathematical objects are under the fictionalist interpretation of mathematics which we discussed in the last chapter. One radical answer to these questions, known under the name of modal realism, has been promulgated by David Lewis. The cornerstone of Lewis's modal realism is the assumption that possible worlds are real, concrete, spatiotemporal collections of particular things. Possible worlds are fundamentally the same types of entities as the actual world. But possible worlds are spatiotemporally and causally isolated from each other. This means that no two things belonging to different possible worlds can stand in any spatiotemporal or causal relation to one another. From the assumption that possible worlds consist of just more things of the same kind as actual things it naturally follows that the notion of actuality of our world has no deeper ontological meaning. The fact that our world is actual does not imply that it is fundamentally and ontologically different from other merely possible worlds. The notion of actuality is in fact relative to the users of language. From the perspective of the inhabitants of a given possible world it is their world which is actual, not ours. This phenomenon is often referred to as the indexical character of actuality. Indexical expressions are terms such as "I", "here", "now", whose meaning and reference change depending on the context of utterance.

Modal realism at first sight seems to be too extravagant to be taken seriously. But Lewis insists that there are good philosophical reasons to adopt such a radical position. The main strength of modal realism lies in its seriously reductive character. Lewis points out that virtually all troublesome types of abstract objects can be reduced in his approach to concrete things and collections thereof. Take for instance the notion of a proposition which we mentioned in the previous chapter. For instance the proposition expressed by the sentence "Paris is the capital of France" is usually assumed to be an abstract, non-spatiotemporal object. But in modal realism this proposition is simply identified with the set of all possible worlds in which Paris is indeed the capital of France. Thus propositions are defined as sets of possible worlds. In this approach the fact that a given proposition P (which is a set of worlds) is true in a world w is concisely expressed in the statement "w is an element of P". A slightly more complex reduction is also possible in the case of properties. A property of, let's say, being green can be defined as the function which assigns to each possible world the set of all its green things. This definition has a clear advantage over the identification of properties with sets of objects in the actual world, because it enables us to differentiate two distinct properties which only happen to be co-extensional (which apply to the same objects in the actual world). Thus the property of having a heart and the property of having kidneys are two different properties, because there are possible worlds in which organisms equipped with hearts don't have kidneys. But some philosophers criticize these reductive definitions for not being entirely adequate. For instance it is often pointed out that all necessary propositions become identical under Lewis's analysis, because they must be identified with the set of all possible worlds.

However, we would like to be able to differentiate between the arithmetical truth "2+2 = 4" and the logical truth "It is snowing or it is not snowing". Similarly, on Lewis's reductive approach the properties of being triangular and being trilateral (having three sides) are presumably identical, as everything which is triangular is necessarily trilateral and vice versa. And yet there are strong intuitions telling us that here we have two distinct but necessarily equivalent properties.

Modal realism has to face yet another difficulty brought about by the need to make identifications of objects from different possible worlds. In order to explicate modal statements involving specific objects (people, places, etc.) we have to assume that other possible worlds can contain objects which are numerically identical with some objects that exist in our world. For instance, in order to account for the statement "Hillary Clinton might have been elected the President of the US in 2008" we should invoke a possible world in which Hillary Clinton exists and has won the election in 2008. But Lewis's conception of possible worlds apparently excludes such a situation from the outset. One and the same object cannot be present in two distinct possible worlds, since this would violate the assumption that possible worlds are spatiotemporally and causally isolated. To deal with this problem, Lewis introduced the notion of a counterpart. Hillary Clinton literally exists in only one world, that is our world, but she has counterparts in other worlds. Counterparts are objects which are sufficiently similar to their originals to play their roles in possible, alternative situations. Presumably, a counterpart of Hillary Clinton would have to be a woman, would have to be born of the same parents, but she could have some properties which the actual Hillary Clinton lacks, such as the property of winning the 2008 presidential election in the USA. Thus a statement about the possibility of a given object possessing a certain property is explicated as saying that in some possible world there is a counterpart of this object which does possess the required property. This explication can, however, be accused of distorting the meaning of the original sentence. When I say that this ten foot high tree could be twelve feet high, I don't want to say that a tree similar to it could be twelve feet high. What I want to say is that this very tree, not its counterpart, might have a different height than it actually has. Lewis's interpretation seems to be unable to differentiate between statements like these: "I could have a different job" and "Someone very much like me could have a different job". But the difference between the two is obvious. I couldn't care less about somebody who is only similar to me. I am only interested in what possibilities apply to me, and not somebody else.

The reductive character of modal realism, which is supposed to be one of its main strengths, turns out to be also the source of a serious shortcoming. On Lewis's approach the modal statement "It is possible that pigs fly" reduces to the statement about the independent and objective existence of some possible worlds – namely the worlds in which it is true that pigs fly. But if those worlds are real spatiotemporal objects which nevertheless are entirely isolated from our world, there is no way for us to acquire any knowledge about their properties and even existence. Consequently, we may never know whether there is indeed a possible world containing flying pigs or not. It looks like Lewis's insistence on the independent existence of isolated possible worlds forces us to become radical skeptics with respect to virtually all modal statements. Our intuitions regarding the truth of even the most basic modal claims may turn out to be entirely inaccurate, and to make matters worse there is no way for us to learn how things really are, because we are forever stuck in our actual world with no access to the realm of objective possibilities.

Given the controversial character of modal realism, it does not come as a surprise that a number of alternative views on the nature of possible worlds have been put forward. Some of them adopt the assumption that possible worlds are mere constructs out of more fundamental objects (Lewis disparagingly refers to this approach as ersatzism, because it replaces genuine possible worlds with ersatz ones). One such conception has been developed by Alvin Plantinga. According to Plantinga possible worlds are special types of states of affairs. This of course calls for an explanation of what states of affairs are. For Plantinga states of affairs are abstract objects corresponding to propositions in a natural way. Some states of affairs are actual, (we say that they "obtain"), but some are not. The states of affairs which obtain correspond to true statements. For instance the state of affairs corresponding to the statement "Paris is the capital of France" obtains, but the state of affairs corresponding to "London is the capital city of France" does not. The distinction between obtaining and not obtaining states of affairs parallels the distinction between exemplified and unexemplified universals accepted by Platonists.

States of affairs exist regardless of whether they obtain or not. A possible world is a state of affairs which is complete (maximal). The condition of maximality can be explained as follows: if a state of affairs S is maximal, then for any other state of affairs, either it is included in S or it is precluded by S. This ensures that possible worlds in Plantinga's approach do not have "gaps" – they are determined in every imaginable aspect. In this approach the actual world can be seen as the only maximal state of affairs which obtains.

As we remember, all explications of modal notions in terms of possible worlds involve the concept of being true in a world. How, then, can we define what it means for a proposition to be true in a particular world if possible worlds are not spatiotemporal wholes but instead abstract states of affairs? Plantinga suggests an ingenious solution to this challenge. He defines the notion of being true in a world in terms of just being true. The notion of truth without any qualification refers to the actual world – the only world that really exists. A sentence is true if it is true in the actual world. But according to Plantinga a sentence P is true in a possible world w, if it is not possible for w to be actual without P being true. Alternatively, we may say that it is necessary that if w were actual (if w obtained), P would be true. It has to be observed, though, that the proposed explication involves the modal notion of possibility (or necessity). But this notion cannot be in turn analyzed in terms of possible worlds, for we would have to invoke "higher level" possible worlds (possible worlds in which a given possible world would be actual). This implies not only that Plantinga's conception of modality is non-reductive (he acknowledges that), but that in fact he needs more than one conceptions of possibility – the usual one, expressed in terms of possible worlds, and an extra notion of possibility used as above.

Plantinga calls his position actualism, because according to it only actual objects exist. Literally there are no possible objects which would not exist in our world. There are no non-existent unicorns, or flying pigs. How, then, can we account for the accepted modal fact that there might have been objects which don't exist? Actualism copes with this problem by resorting to properties, which are assumed to exist in the actual world. Plantinga argues that each actual object possesses its unique essence: the property that is necessarily possessed by this and only this object. For instance, there is the property of being Hillary Clinton which is her essential property, and no person other than Hillary Clinton can possess it. However, there

54

can be essences which are not exemplified in the actual world but may be exemplified in other possible worlds. Thus the statement "Flying pigs may exist" is true if there is a possible world in which some essence is coexemplified with the property of being a flying pig. The apparent advantage of this solution is that it assumes the literal existence of properties only, which according to Plantinga are necessary beings. However, it is unclear what his intended interpretation of the relation of coexemplification (co-instantiation) should be. It cannot be interpreted literally, since this would imply that there is an object which possesses the property of being a flying pig, and the actualist cannot accept that, for flying pigs are not actual objects. It looks like exemplification and coexemplification have to be treated as primitive terms, but this reliance on a growing number of primitive unanalyzable terms seriously undermines the attractiveness of the entire doctrine.

Necessity and identity

The last topic covered in this chapter will be the modal status of identity statements. Does the relation of numerical identity hold contingently or necessarily between its arguments? Taking into account the example discussed in Chapter 1 in connection with Frege's worries about the informativeness of identity claims, we may suspect that some of these claims should be contingent, and not necessary. The identity "the Morning Star = the Evening Star" tells us something about the world which we couldn't find out by simply studying the meanings of words. Frege insisted that the two names on both sides of the equality sign differ in meaning, and hence the identity between their referents has to be verified by non-linguistic means (for instance empirically). This may suggest that the Morning Star could in fact be a different object than the Evening Star; that it only happened contingently that the two names refer to one and the same celestial body. But the logician and philosopher Saul Kripke, who laid the foundations for the modern semantics of modality, made the astonishing claim that all true identity statements are necessary. Kripke offered a simple formal argument in support of his claim. The first premise of the argument is that every object is necessarily identical with itself: for all x, it is necessarily true that $x = x$. Now let us assume that for some objects x and y, x is identical with y. From Leibniz's law, which is a law of logic (see Chapter 1) it follows that if in any true statement containing variable x we replace this variable with another variable y of which we assume that $x = y$, the resulting statement will remain true. Using this fact we can now replace one occurrence of variable x in the first premise by y, thus obtaining the following true conditional statement: for all x and y, if $x = y$, then it is necessarily true that $x = y$. Hence, if identity holds between objects x and y, it holds necessarily.

The conclusion of the aforesaid argument may be seen as quite trivial and innocuous. After all, as Kripke himself pointed out, the expression "For all y, if $x = y$, then y has property P" is just a long-winded version of a much simpler statement "x has property P". To see this, compare "John is tall" with "Whoever is identical with John, is tall". So obviously, if x is necessarily identical with x, then whatever is identical with x, is also necessarily identical with x. But now we can use the well-known law of logic which allows replacing all variables bound by universal quantifiers with any names of our choice. This law, known as universal instantiation, legitimizes for instance the following inference: If all presidents of the US have been males, then Barack Obama is male (given that he's president). When we apply this rule to our case, we can conclude that if $a = b$, then $a = b$ is necessarily true, where a and b are any names. But this is surprising. Surely the Morning Star is identical with the Evening Star, but is this necessarily so? We can clearly imagine a possible world in which the bright object observed after sunset is the planet Venus, whereas the similar looking object appearing just before dusk is a different thing, for instance planet X. Doesn't this possible world falsify the claim of the necessary character of the considered identity statement? Kripke thinks not. He insists that the world described above is not a world in which the Morning Star is not identical with the Evening Star. The Morning Star and the Evening Star are just two names of the same object: the planet Venus. In any possible world if they refer to anything at all, it is the same object. However, as Frege noted, in our world the two names are (contingently) associated with different descriptions which serve as a way to pick their referent. In other worlds this may not be the case, and that's why we may wrongly think that the appropriate identity doesn't hold. Indeed, in the possible world considered above, the reference of the name "Morning Star" is no longer fixed by the description "the brightest object in the early morning sky". The Morning Star still refers to Venus and not planet X, which in this world satisfies the description. Kripke's analysis of identity statements can be concisely presented using his own notion of rigid designator. To remind you, a rigid designator is an expression which refers to the same object in every possible world (if it refers to anything in that world). Unquestionably, if a and b are rigid designators, then it trivially follows that if $a = b$ is true in the actual world, this identity has to hold in all possible worlds. When applied to rigid designators, the thesis of the necessity of identity becomes indeed trivial. However, what is not trivial is Kripke's claim that typical names used in natural language, such as "the Morning Star", function as rigid designators. Among non-rigid designators, on the other hand, are descriptions, such as "The tallest person in town". Suppose the tallest person in some town happens to be one John Smith. That the name "John Smith", as opposed to the above description, is a rigid designator, can be seen when we consider the modal statement "John Smith might not be the tallest person in town". This statement is considered true if there is a possible world in which the very same John Smith is not the tallest person in town. On the other hand, the sentence "The tallest person in town might not be the tallest person in town" is patently false. To evaluate it, we look in any possible world at whoever happens to be the tallest person in town, and of course she/he can't fail to have this property.

Kripke's insistence on the necessary character of identity statements involving proper names has important consequences for the status of a special type of scientific identifications. In science it is commonplace to identify certain categories of objects or phenomena with some other kinds. For instance thermodynamics identifies heat as the motion of molecules, and chemistry states that water is a substance composed of H_2O molecules. It may seem that such identities express contingent facts about our world. After all, water might have turned out to have a different chemical structure, and heat might have been produced by an entirely different internal mechanism. But the previous arguments show that this is actually impossible. Water is made of H_2O in all possible worlds, and the term "heat" always refers to the internal motion of molecules. Our "illusion of contingency" comes from the fact that we can clearly imagine a world in which the "watery" stuff filling the oceans and quenching our thirst is not H_2O, and another world in which the sensation of heat is produced by something else rather than the motion of molecules. But these are not worlds in which appropriate identities fail to hold, but rather worlds in which our methods of fixing reference of certain general terms are no longer valid. Thus we can no longer identify water using the description of its color, smell, etc., and we can't say that what produces the sensation of heat is really heat. So Kripke admits that water might have different perceptual qualities, and heat might produce different sensations. But once we use the contingent association of the terms "water" and "heat" with appropriate descriptions in our world, the reference of these terms is fixed and cannot change across possible worlds.

A special case of identification which deserves particular attention can be found in the philosophy of mind. According to the so-called identity theory, mental processes and events are actually identical with certain physical processes. For instance, it is theorized that the sensation of pain is nothing more than a particular electrical excitation of certain types of neurons. Moreover, identity theorists must assume that this identification is contingent only, because we can clearly imagine an organism physically identical with a human body and yet without any mental states (a so-called "zombie"). But we already know that this can't be right. The term "pain" is a rigid designator that refers in all possible worlds to the same type of neuronal processes (at least according to the identity theory). However, the proponents of the theory may counteract by saying that at least it is possible that the way we identify pain in our world may not be applicable in another world. But is this really an option? Kripke points out that the term "pain" is peculiar in that the only method of fixing its referent is by referring to pain itself. Compare this with the case of heat. In our world we fix its reference by applying the description "that which produces the sensation of heat". Because in our world it is the motion of molecules which is causally responsible for our sensation, the reference is thus determined, but in other possible worlds the same sensation may be associated with a totally different physical cause. But in the case of pain the description corresponding to the term is "the sensation of pain", and it is essentially the same as the term itself. You can't have pain without feeling pain. That way Kripke argues that the identity theory turns out to be inconsistent.

But perhaps the identity theorists could hold their ground by zooming in on the second element of their identification rather than the first. The term "c-fiber firing", which is typically used to describe the purported physical process underlying pain, is associated in our world with a certain way of identifying its referent by observing electrical impulses passing through the neuronal web. It may be claimed that in our world the reference of this term is actually fixed on the sensation of pain, and that this term in other possible worlds should refer to the same type of mental states. However, now it is perfectly possible that the term "c-fiber firing", conceived as a rigid designator, will not be associated with our typical way of fixing its reference in other possible worlds. Thus, it may be maintained that it is a contingent fact that the process which in any possible world we identify as corresponding to a particular flow of electricity through the neuronal web is actually identical with the feeling of pain.

4 TIME AND TEMPORAL OBJECTS

Time and temporality have always been at the center of metaphysical investigations. Today's metaphysics of time is strongly influenced by the advances of modern science (mostly physics), but it still remains an independent and active area of philosophical research. In this chapter we will see how philosophers try to capture the essence of the temporal character of the physical world. Some of them insist that temporality can be analyzed exclusively in terms of an ordering of events, whereas others maintain that there is yet another aspect of time which has to be taken into account – the so-called passage of time. The proponents of the objective passage of time usually believe that what is happening now is somehow ontologically privileged in comparison with what will happen or what has happened. On the other hand, this special ontological character of the present is questioned by those who want to reduce time to a mere succession of events. We will see how modern physical theories, such as special relativity, bear on this issue. The special and general theories of relativity have an impact on yet another fundamental debate regarding the nature of time (and space as well). The question considered here is whether time and space are entities independent of physical objects, or do they owe their existence to more fundamental beings. Finally, we will briefly touch upon the subject of how things persist in time. However, we will start our discussion on time with an introduction and analysis of another crucial ontological category – that of events.

Events

Events are assumed to form a category of spatiotemporal objects which is separate from the category of things. Although both events and things exist in space and time, their modes of spatiotemporality are significantly distinct. Things are considered to be *continuants*, which means that even though they exist throughout longer periods of time, at each particular moment a given thing is fully and completely present. Events, on the other hand, are *occurents*. They are not complete until the last moment of their existence. To illustrate this distinction, let us compare Napoleon (ontologically speaking, a thing) with the Battle of Waterloo (an event). Both Napoleon and the battle coexisted during a certain period of time, but at each moment of the battle Napoleon existed as a complete entity, whereas the same moment contained only a small fragment of the entire battle. It has to be added, though, that there is a non-standard interpretation available according to which things exist in time in a similar way to events. We will talk more about this suggestion later in the chapter.

Events are commonly used in natural language as well as the language of science and philosophy. We talk without reservation about battles, treaties, births, deaths, earthquakes, hurricanes, and so on. Fundamental physics is chock-full of reference to events: collisions, annihilations, creations, absorptions, emissions. In philosophy events are considered to be proper arguments of the causal relation. We also talk about mental events, actions and beliefs. Thus the ontological thesis about the reality of events seems to be well supported by linguistic practice. But for those still unconvinced we may offer an additional linguistic argument, originally formulated by Donald Davidson. Consider the following sentence: (P) Jones is slowly buttering his toast with a knife in the kitchen. It is obvious that sentence (P) logically implies that Jones is buttering his toast, that Jones is doing something with a knife in the kitchen, and so on. However, it turns out that it is rather difficult to formalize these unquestionable inferences in a language which assumes the existence of things only. This is so because standard logic does not offer a straightforward way of representing adverbial modifications (such as "slowly" or "in the kitchen") as separate parts of predicates. On the other hand, if we introduce events into our domain, we can rephrase all the sentences involved in such a way that the logical entailment will be clearly visible. The starting sentence (P) can be interpreted as:

(Q) There is an event x such that x is a buttering of toast, x is done by Jones, x is done slowly, x is done with a knife, x is done in the kitchen. Now all adverbial modifications are transformed into predicates attributed to one event: the buttering. And by eliminating various elements of the entire conjunction we can derive all the required consequences using the well-known logical law which enables us to infer each conjunct from a conjunction of two or more sentences.

Once we have accepted events into our ontology, we should formulate some criteria of their identity and distinctness. When can we say that we have two events rather than one? One possible answer may be that two events are identical if they coincide spatiotemporally. But there are convincing examples of events which violate this rule. Imagine a metal sphere which is rotating around its axis and at the same time is heating up. The events of rotating and of heating up are intuitively distinct, and yet they occupy the same area of space-time. One way of dealing with this challenge is to adopt the criterion proposed by Davidson, according to which events are numerically identical if and only if they have exactly the same causes and the same effects. Clearly the sphere's rotation and its heating up have different causes and effects (for instance the former causes the sphere to flatten a bit at the poles, whereas the latter causes it to expand uniformly). But there is one big problem with the Davidsonian criterion. In order to decide whether an event x is identical with an event y we have to identify and compare all causes and effects for x and y. But in order to verify whether a given cause for x is the same as a cause of y we must use the same criterion again, and it prescribes that we have to determine first whether x and y are identical or not (as x and y are effects of the events considered). Thus we are going in a circle: in order to decide whether x is identical with y we should know in advance whether they are identical or not. It is generally accepted that Davidson's criterion cannot avoid the circularity problem, even though in some special cases a proper identification of two events can be made on its basis.

In the light of this difficulty, another interpretation of events has been proposed by Jaegwon Kim. Events for Kim are property exemplifications, or more specifically triples of the form $\langle a, P, t \rangle$, where a is an object, P is a property, and t is a time at which a possesses P. From this characteristic it follows that two events are identical when they occur on the same object, at the same time, and involve the same property. The last condition ensures that the rotation and the heating up of a sphere are numerically distinct events. But Kim's conception of events has several controversial consequences. First of all, it multiplies events beyond what is usually seen as necessary. If Jones is walking slowly, his walking and his walking slowly constitute two numerically distinct events, since the properties involved in each event are numerically different. Moreover, under this interpretation events become extremely fragile. This means that the conditions of numerical identity for events are so strict that a small and supposedly insignificant change can lead to the utter loss of identity of a given event. We may for instance ask whether it is possible for a given event to happen a moment earlier or later. It turns out that such a change would most probably lead to a new event, since the time of occurrence is an essential feature of events under Kim's analysis. Similarly, a rotation of a sphere which is slightly faster than the actual one cannot be numerically identical with it. Consequently, intuitively true modal sentences such as "This lecture might have started a minute earlier" or "This rotation of the sphere might have been a bit faster" come out false under Kim's interpretation. The fragility of events has other important consequences for the issue of causality, as we will see in the next chapter.

For the purpose of the analysis of time and temporal properties it will be convenient to select a particular category of events, which we can call "point-like" events. These are events that don't have any spatial or temporal dimensions (they occupy one point of space and time). Obviously events of that sort are idealizations, but they are quite useful. One important advantage of using point-like events is that it is easy to put them in a temporal order without running into the problem of how to account for events that only partially overlap each other. With point-like events the situation is clear: either two events wholly coincide temporarily (they occur at the same time) or one of them is unambiguously earlier than the other. This is also much simpler in comparison with various temporal relations in which things may stand to each other. During their histories things may temporarily overlap, the temporal history of one may be fully included in the history of the other, and so on. But this is not so with point-like events.

63

Temporal relations

The fundamental temporal relation is that of temporal ordering. We order events in time by putting them side by side from earlier to later ones, like we do with historical events on a timeline. Let us focus our attention on the earlier-than relation. It is easy to observe that this relation possesses the following formal features. First of all, obviously no event can occur earlier than itself. We call relations which never hold between an object and itself irreflexive (the opposite notion of reflexivity was introduced in Chapter 1). In addition to that we may observe that the earlier-than relation is asymmetric, i.e. if event *x* is earlier than event *y*, *y* can't be earlier than *x*. Finally, temporal ordering is transitive. If Julius Caesar's death happened earlier than the fall of Constantinople, and the fall of Constantinople temporally precedes the Battle of Trafalgar, then clearly Julius Caesar's death must be earlier than the Battle of Trafalgar. But the combined properties of irreflexivity, asymmetry and transitivity may not be sufficient to fully characterize the type of ordering represented by the earlier-than relation. We want to ensure that temporally ordered events form one single line, and not a branching tree. It is easy to notice that the relation which orders events on a tree, where events located on different branches are simply incomparable with one another, still satisfy all three characteristics given above. To eliminate such a situation, a new condition of linearity must be introduced. This can be done as follows. First, let us define a new and important relation: that of simultaneity. Two events may be characterized as simultaneous when one is neither earlier nor later than the other. We should expect the relation of simultaneity to be an equivalence relation, i.e. to be reflexive, symmetric and transitive (you can check the definitions of these terms in Chapter 1). And indeed when we impose the condition of being an equivalence relation on simultaneity defined as above, the linearity property will follow. It can be quickly verified that in the case of a branching time the relation of simultaneity is not transitive, and hence not an equivalence relation.

With the equivalence relation of simultaneity at our disposal, we can now define a new and important category of temporal objects: moments (instants). A moment can be characterized as the set of all events which are simultaneous with one another. The moment at which a given event *x* occurs is obviously the set of all events

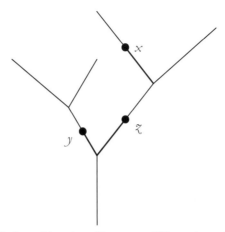

An example of a branching time. Events on different branches are not comparable with one another with respect to their temporal order. Simultaneity defined as being neither earlier nor later than is not transitive: x is "simultaneous" with y and y is "simultaneous" with z, but x is later than z.

simultaneous with x. The relation of being earlier than can be naturally extended from events onto moments. Moment m is considered to be earlier than moment n if all events constituting m are earlier than events composing n. We can observe that the relation of simultaneity defined on moments reduces simply to numerical identity. The only moment simultaneous with m is m itself. For that reason moments satisfy the condition known as connectivity: for all non-identical moments m and n, either m is earlier than n, or n is earlier than m. It has to be stressed that the way we have introduced moments presupposes that there can be no "empty" moments (moments at which no event takes place). However, this assumption is subject to a philosophical controversy which will be analyzed later in this chapter.

With the help of the qualitative earlier-than relation we can only make crude comparisons between events. To make the temporal characteristic of events more precise, a numerical measure of temporal intervals is necessary. We have no room here to present the details of how measurable properties of time should be introduced. However, we may note that the key point is to define what it means for two temporal intervals to be of the same length. An interval is defined simply by two events: its beginning and its end. To compare the lengths of two intervals defined by events *a*, *b* and by events *c*, *d*, we need to apply a common measure. This measure is typically a cyclic process (such as the rotation of the Earth, or the pulsation of an atomic clock). The intervals are considered equal in length (duration) if the same numbers of cycles fit in both of them. However, a conceptual problem arises here. How do we know that the cycles used in a particular measuring mechanism are indeed of the same duration? In order to verify this, we would have to resort to another cyclic process, but now the question can be repeated, which leads to a regress. A solution to this problem suggested by some philosophers is that ultimately we have to rely on a conventional decision. The convention adopted should be such that the laws of nature involving the measure of time should have the simplest form possible. For instance, it makes sense to adopt a definition of equal intervals according to which an object moving freely in space will cover equal distances in equal units of time (the first law of dynamics).

So far our analysis of temporal relations has been done entirely within the framework of classical physics. But it is a well-known fact that the introduction of the special theory of relativity changed dramatically our way of describing temporal connections between events. Special relativity is based on the fundamental assumption that the speed of light is always the same for all observers (in all frames of reference). One important consequence of this assumption is that the relation of simultaneity becomes dependent on the choice of a frame of reference (in the special theory of relativity we only consider inertial, that is non-accelerating frames). More precisely, if two events are simultaneous in one frame of reference (for instance the frame of reference associated with the Earth's surface) they will usually not be simultaneous in another frame of reference moving with respect to the first one (let's say the frame of reference defined by a passing train). This follows directly from the way simultaneity is defined in physics: two events are deemed simultaneous if beams of light sent from both of them meet exactly half way between those events. If this condition is satisfied with respect to one frame of reference, and we consider another frame moving uniformly in the direction of one event, the point at which the two beams meet will not fall in the middle of the distance between the events as measured in the second frame. Thus from the perspective of the second frame the event

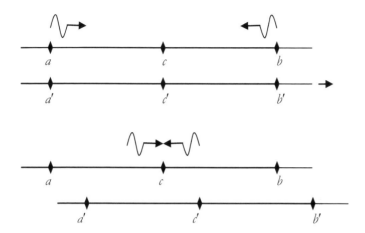

Relativity of simultaneity. Two beams of light meet exactly half-way in the unprimed frame of reference, but not in the primed frame which moves to the right.

towards which the frame is moving happened earlier than the other one.

One immediate consequence of this fact is that when we want to put events in a temporal order, we have to state explicitly with respect to what frame this is to be done. Thus there is not a single earlier-than relation ordering events, but as many as there are different frames of reference. Even more surprisingly, the notion of a moment has to be relativized in an analogous way. There is no single, absolute moment at which a given event takes place. A moment is a set of simultaneous events, but which events are simultaneous with a given one depends on the selected frame of reference. Thus an event *x* happens at some moment *m* with respect to one frame of reference, but at a numerically different moment *m'* (because it contains different events than those in *m*) in another frame of reference. Moments *m* and *m'* are not even comparable with one another (it doesn't make sense to ask which one is earlier). Moments can be temporally compared only when they are defined in the same frame of reference. Thus instead of using the term "moment" we should actually apply the longer term "moment-in-a-given-frame", and similarly instead of introducing one relation of earlier than, we should talk about the earlier-than-in-a-given-frame relation.

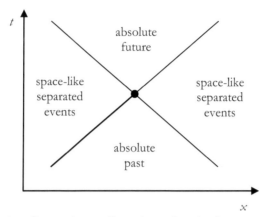

Space-time diagram in two dimensions. Crossing lines represent trajectories of light beams. Events from the absolute future and the absolute past can be connected with the central event by slower-than-light signals. Events space-like separated from the centre cannot be reached by subluminal signals.

However, not everything is relative in the special theory of relativity. It is possible to introduce new relations between events which will hold in all frames of reference. Such relations are called absolute. But as it turns out they are no longer purely temporal, but rather spatiotemporal. All these relations can be defined with the help of light signals. One of them can be called "being in the absolute (causal) past of". This relation holds between events x and y if a signal travelling at a speed lower than or equal to the speed of light and sent from x can reach event y. This definition is clearly independent of the choice of frame of reference, because if the speed of a signal is lower than the speed of light in one frame, this remains true in all frames. The converse of this relation gives us the relation of being in the absolute causal future. And the third important absolute relation is in a sense the complement of the above two. It is known as space-like separation (whereas the remaining two relations can be jointly characterized as time-like or light-like separation). Two events are space-like separated if there is no signal travelling at or below the speed of light which could connect them. All these relations can be conveniently presented on space-time diagrams. It may be interesting to know that they can also be defined in terms of relative relations of earlier then and being simultaneous with. For instance, x is absolutely in the past of y if in all frames of reference x is earlier than y. And x is space-like separated from y, if there is a frame of reference in which x is simultaneous with y.

The A-series and the B-series

After this brief excursion into physics let us return to philosophy. Some philosophers believe that all there is to time, metaphysically speaking, is included in the temporal ordering given by the earlier-than relation. But others disagree. One important aspect that is supposedly missing from the account of time in terms of a temporal order is the distinction between the three spheres of time: the past, the present, and the future. It is customary to use the terms "A-series" and "B-series", introduced by the British philosopher John McTaggart who worked at the turn of the 19th and 20th centuries, to differentiate between the two interpretations of time that emerge here. The A-series can be characterized as the set of all events separated into past, present, and future ones. On the other hand, the B-series contains events which are ordered with the help of the earlier-than relation. No distinction between the past, the present and the future is made in the characterization of the B-series. McTaggart stresses that one crucial difference between these two concepts of time is that the B-series is in a sense static, whereas the A-series is dynamic. That is to say, if an event x in the B-series is earlier than another event y, they "remain" temporarily ordered in that way for eternity, whereas events in the A-series continuously change their status from being future, to being present, and then past. Consequently, in order to describe the B-series we can use a tenseless language in which we employ only the present-tense form of verbs. For instance, it is perfectly acceptable to say that Caesar's death *is* earlier than the Battle of Hastings (not: *was* earlier, or *will be* earlier, or *is being* earlier now). On the other hand, tensed verbs are necessary in order to speak about the A-series. The Battle of Hastings is past now, but it was present, and even earlier it was also future, whereas your reading this sentence is present now, but was future and will be past.

Famously, McTaggart made two claims regarding the interpretations of time introduced above. His first claim is that the existence of an A-series is necessary for time to exist. In other words, the B-series in itself is not sufficient for time to emerge. But the second claim is that the A-series is in fact self-contradictory, and hence cannot exist. Putting these two theses together, McTaggart concludes that time does not exist, and our experience of temporality is just an illusion. We will analyze these claims separately, starting with the first one. The argument for the indispensable character of the A-series consists of two steps. First, McTaggart argues that there is no time without change. For the moment we will not contest this claim, leaving it for a later time. But the second step deserves our close attention. McTaggart insists that change can occur only within the A-series, not the B-series. This claim is a consequence of the way he defines what change is. For McTaggart the only phenomenon which deserves to be called change is the alteration of the temporal status of events from being future, through being present to being past. Clearly, this type of change can only happen in the A-series, since the B-series doesn't even introduce the talk about the past, present and the future (at least not in a non-relativized form). But critics point out that McTaggart's notion of change is not the only one imaginable. Bertrand Russell for instance observes that properly speaking only things can alter, not events. And a thing changes if it possesses a certain property at one time, and ceases to possess this property at a later time. For instance a poker can alter its state from being hot at some moment t to being cold at a later moment t'. Certainly this type of change does not need anything more than the existence of a B-series with its earlier-than relation.

It is instructive to see how McTaggart reacts to this challenge. Predictably, he accuses the Russellian notion of change of being spurious. For McTaggart no real change takes place in the poker example, since it is always true that the poker is hot at t and cold at t', thus the involved facts are eternal and immutable. To bolster his claim, he uses an argument from analogy. Let us consider the Prime Meridian and two points on it: one located in France, and the other in England. The points on the meridian can be ordered analogously to the temporal points (for instance in the direction from the South Pole to the North Pole), so we can say that according to such an ordering the selected point in France is "earlier" than the point in England. But now McTaggart observes that the sentence "This point is in France" is true at the first point but false at the second one, in analogy with the poker case, where the sentence "The poker is hot" is true at moment t but false at t'. And yet there is no change in the meridian example. By analogy, no alteration should occur in the case involving temporal points either.

McTaggart's argument can be questioned on the ground of an insufficient analogy between the temporal case and the spatial case. First, we may observe that the meridian example lacks a clear counterpart of the thing which remains the same during the change (the poker). The role of such a thing can't be played by the meridian itself, which instead is an analogue of the sequence of moments. Moreover, it may be claimed that the fact that we can artificially order points on a meridian does not mean that the selected ordering reflects some objective, independently existing relation. For instance, it doesn't really matter whether we order points from the south to the north or from the north to the south. On the other hand, one can argue that there is an objective, ontological difference between being earlier than and being later than. This difference is sometimes described as following from the objectivity of time's arrow (we will discuss this point later in this chapter). As McTaggart's rebuttal of Russell's example is based on a weak analogy, its conclusion can be legitimately questioned.

But for now let us move on to his second argument, which presents an even greater interpretational challenge. The argument for the thesis that the A-series is contradictory begins with the unquestionable premise that the three spheres of past, present and future events are mutually exclusive. But McTaggart surprisingly asserts that in spite of this we have to assume that each event is past, present and future. This announcement can certainly cause a few raised eyebrows. One is tempted to respond to McTaggart that events are not past, present and future simultaneously, but in succession. For instance the Battle of Hastings is past, but was present, and had been future before it actually began. And my current typing is present, but was future and will be past. But McTaggart demands that we explain precisely what we mean by the tensed forms of the verb "be". The tensed forms of verbs can be explained only with the help of the A-series notions of being past, present and future. One such explication may go as follows. An event x *was* present means that x is present at some past moment (where "is" is used in a tenseless sense). An event x *will be* past means that x is past at some future moment. Those explications presuppose that the distinction can be made between past, present, and future moments, and McTaggart's question can be repeated with respect to them. That is, in order to avoid an immediate contradiction we have to assume that some moments are past at a present moment, present at a past moment, and future at another past moment, and so on. But here we have to rely on "second-level" moments, and with respect to these moments the same problem returns all over again, which requires an introduction of third-level moments, fourth-level moments, etc. This looks like a dangerous regress to infinity.

Some commentators maintain that this regress can be avoided. For instance Jonathan Lowe claims that we don't need to introduce multileveled moments in order to express the properties of the A-series. Instead of explicating tensed forms "was present", "will be past", etc. in terms of past, present and future moments, we can resort to adverbial modifications: "is pastly present", "is futurely past". Lowe insists that the division of events into nine categories obtained by combining the adverbs "pastly", "presently" and "futurely" with terms "past", "present" and "future" is all we need to speak consistently about the A-series without the fear of an infinite regress. But this can be doubted. The central point of McTaggart's argument, as I see it, is that the A-series has to be dynamic, not static. A mere division into past, present and future events does not make time "flow", for we can easily categorize events into those three classes and keep them there "forever". That is why McTaggart insists that each event has to have a chance to go through all three stages. But how can we express this thought without falling victim to a contradiction or an infinite regress? The new terms introduced by Lowe only add more categories to the picture, without turning it from static to dynamic. Actually, it can be easily observed that the nine new categories are reducible to the old categories of past, present and future events. For instance events which are presently past are just past, and events which are pastly future are those which are present or future. So if the three initial categories are not sufficient for the A-series, it is doubtful that the nine new ones will do the job. Lowe may respond that the term "a futurely past event" when applied to a present event implies that this event will at a certain moment in the future change from present into past. But to warrant this inference we have to analyze first what it means to be futurely past, and as McTaggart showed, such an analysis can never be completed. And if we treat the term "futurely past" as a further unanalyzable unit, we cannot support the above intuitive reasoning.

The passage of time

The dilemma posed by McTaggart gives rise to two opposite views regarding the nature of time. Those who accept the first argument for the indispensability of the A-series but reject the second argument which questions its consistency are labeled A-theorists. On the other hand, B-theorists are happy to embrace the consequence of the second argument, but deny that we really need an A-series at all. (It has to be added, though, that some philosophers sympathetic to the A-theory nevertheless agree with McTaggart that any attempt to express the essential properties of the A-series is doomed to fail. But they believe that this only goes to show the limitations of our conceptual framework, and not that time itself is unreal. Michael Dummett is one of those philosophers.) The B-theorists mount an attack on the notion of the passage of time. They believe that nothing in reality corresponds to our perception of time's flowing, or events' passing. The B-theorists Donald Williams and J.J.C. Smart give the following arguments against the reality of time's passage. First of all, they note that all attempts to properly describe what the flow of time is end invariably with some metaphor which cannot possibly be taken literally. For instance C.D. Broad, a British philosopher, made a comparison of the passage of time to a policeman carrying a torch and moving alongside a row of houses. At each moment his torch shines on one house only, and this is supposed to represent the moving now. Another analogy used in the context of time is a movie projector and two rolls of film which constantly unwind and wind. One roll represents the future events, the other the past ones, and the moving present is just the frame which is currently projected on the screen. But when we try to express these intuitions in a more precise language, we encounter fundamental obstacles.

Williams notes that if we took the idea of the flow of time literally, it would make sense to ask how fast it is. But the rate of time's flow would have to be measured in seconds per seconds, and this gives a dimensionless quantity, which is absurd. Moreover, the movement of the objective now requires a second-level time in which it is performed. When we speak about an object moving in space, we assume that its spatial location at one moment is different than the location at another. Similarly, in order to account for the passage of the objective present along the temporal line, we would have to introduce a new category of moments in order to say that the present is located in different places on the timeline (defined by ordinary, first-order moments) at different second-order moments. But the second-order moments presumably also participate in the passage of time, and hence require the third-order moments, and so on. This regress looks quite similar to the one presented in McTaggart's argument.

However, these arguments are far from being decisive. Tim Maudlin, for instance, claims that the "seconds per seconds" objection misses the point. According to him there is nothing wrong with dimensionless quantities. For instance the rate of exchange of one currency into itself is given by a dimensionless quantity (e.g. dollars per dollars). Nonetheless, it is still quite unsettling that the rate of the flow of time can assume only one value (one second per second). This means that time can neither speed up nor slow down. But Peter Forrest disagrees with that. In his interpretation the passage of time is the process in which new layers of space-time of non-zero thickness are being added to the already existing universe. The rate of the flow of time is given by the thickness of the successive layers, which means that the thicker they are, the faster time flows. However, this approach has one unintuitive consequence. If we consider the limit case in which the flow of time is realized by adding just one spatiotemporal layer of an infinite thickness which contains the entire history of the universe, the rate of the passage of time should also be considered infinite. But on the other hand this situation looks very much like a universe in which there is no passage of time at all, and thus the rate of flow is zero.

One of the main challenges for the B-theory of time is how to account for the use of tensed verbs and other temporal expressions in the tenseless language of the B-series. What sense can we make of expressions such as "yesterday", "ten days ago", "now", "in a second" if they cannot be interpreted as presupposing an objective distinction between the ever moving present, the growing past and the shrinking future? A typical response by the B-theorists is that such expressions are indexical, that is their meaning depends on the moment of utterance. So the word "yesterday" should be read "one day before the moment of this utterance", and "The Battle of Hastings is past" is interpreted as "The Battle of Hastings is earlier than the moment of this utterance". B-theorists draw an analogy between temporal expressions and spatial expressions, such as "here", "there", "ten meters south-east from here", etc. When I say "here" when standing in Trafalgar Square, this word has a different reference than when I utter it while in Times Square. But there is nothing special about my "here" other than that it happens to be the place I currently occupy. So why should my "now" be in any way privileged? The only fact that makes my present special is that my consciousness happens to occupy this particular moment. But there is one problem with this answer. Consciousness is not momentary, but has some duration covering almost the entire life of an individual. The stages of my consciousness occupy an extended period of time, which according to common sense contains past, present, and future moments. What is it, then, that differentiates my current "now" from my past "nows" and my future "nows"?

The B-theory of time combines naturally with a particular position regarding the reality of temporal spheres of events, called eternalism (or the block universe view). According to eternalism, all events – past, present, and future – exist in the same fundamental sense. That is to say, past events such as the Battle of Hastings have not vanished but are real in the same way as the events that we perceive as present. Even future events are real, although we cannot have any causal contact with them yet. The entire universe is a four-dimensional block with three spatial dimensions and one temporal. Events that are separated by a non-zero temporal interval exist in the same way as events that are separated spatially. But some philosophers point out that this view, even though in line with modern scientific theories, has some unintuitive consequences. The philosopher and logician Arthur Prior has developed a simple and yet powerful argument against eternalism. He observes that the eternalist cannot satisfactorily explain why we feel relieved when a bad and painful experience has come to an end. For instance, when my teeth stop aching after taking a pain killer, I may breathe a sigh of relief "Thanks goodness that's over". But why should I feel happy that my pain is gone if it exists for eternity in some temporal sphere of reality? Surely the response adumbrated by eternalists "I feel relieved because the moment of my pain is earlier from the moment of this utterance" looks absurd. I feel relieved because I don't feel pain anymore, and not because of any temporal relation that holds between some events whose existence is not questioned.

The A-theory is compatible with more than one view regarding the reality of the past and the future. However, typically it is associated with the view known as presentism, according to which only present events and things exist. The universe consists just of one three-dimensional layer of simultaneous events which "moves" as time passes. Presentism is threatened by two arguments: one from physics and one from semantics. Let us take up the semantic objection first. It is intuitively obvious that there are plenty of true sentences about past events and things (and perhaps even about future events and things). But how can these sentences be true if what they are about (i.e. past or future objects) does not exist? Consider for instance the sentence "Napoleon was short". According to presentism, Napoleon does not belong to the most comprehensive domain of our language, since this domain can contain only present objects, and Napoleon is clearly not present. But how can a true sentence be about a non-existent object? Some presentists reply to this challenge by appealing to the *de re – de dicto* distinction which we introduced in Chapter 3. The sentence "Napoleon was short" admits two interpretations. In the *de re* interpretation it states that there is someone who is Napoleon and has the property of being short in the past. This sentence is clearly false under presentism, since there is no-one now who is identical with Napoleon. But the *de dicto* interpretation is weaker. It only states that it was true that a person called Napoleon was short. Such a sentence does not commit us to the existence of Napoleon, since it is no longer true that Napoleon is short. This situation is perfectly analogous to the modal case in which we make a distinction between the *de re* sentence "There is a person who might have been the female president of the US in 2008" and the *de dicto* expression "It might have been the case that someone was the female president of the US in 2008". For the presentist the expressions "It was the case that" and "It will be the case that" are just analogous to the *de dicto* modal term "it is possible that".

However, the question of the proper semantics for sentences involving the operators "it was (will be) the case that" may be raised. As we remember, in the modal case the semantics is based on the framework of possible worlds, which may be interpreted either as spatiotemporal concrete wholes (Lewis) or as abstract states of affairs (Plantinga). It should be clear that in the case of statements about the past and future the Lewisian option is not available to the presentist, since it would amount to admitting that past and future events exist. Thus the most natural option for the presentist is to follow the example of actualism. The statement "It was the case that Napoleon was short" is considered true when the individual essence of

Napoleon (which is a property existing now) is coexemplified in the past with the property of being short. Again, as in the case of modal actualism, we have to assume that the relation of "coexemplification in the past" is primitive, as it cannot be explicated within the conceptual framework of presentism.

The physical argument against presentism is based on the special theory of relativity. According to presentism only events that happen at the present time exist. But what is the present time precisely? Surely it should consist of events which are simultaneous with one another – if one event is earlier than another, they can't both be present. But we have already learned that according to the special theory of relativity the relation of simultaneity is frame-dependent. That is, if a distant event is simultaneous with my current state of consciousness, this event will not be simultaneous with my present state in another frame of reference. Yet an event cannot exist in one frame of reference, and not exist in another. Thus presentism is committed to the existence of a special, privileged frame of reference which defines the absolute plane of simultaneity. However, precisely the existence of such a privileged frame is denied by relativity theory. One possible reply to this argument is that actually the existence of a privileged frame of reference is not incompatible with relativistic physics. What is really incompatible is the thesis that there could be some physical, measurable effects which would differentiate such a frame from all the other ones. So the presentist can maintain that one such frame is indeed ontologically privileged by the very fact that it defines an objective sphere of present events. However, no physical effect can indeed single out this particular frame.

There are two more views that can be seen as springing from the A-theory of time. One of them is called the growing block view, and according to it only the spheres of past and present events exist. The universe is a four-dimensional whole which constantly grows, and the three-dimensional layer that tops it is the ever-moving present. The mirror-image of this view is the shrinking block conception, which assumes that the universe consists of present and future events, and it diminishes in its temporal extent as time passes. It has to be noted that these two views inherit most problems of both eternalism and presentism without adding any obvious new advantages. For instance, they are open to the "Thanks goodness that's over" objection or a variant thereof, and still run counter to the special theory of relativity.

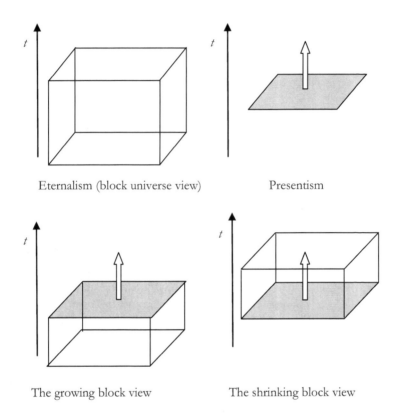

Four views on the existence of temporal spheres.

Absolutism and relationism

In this section we will consider the question of the ontological status of time and its relation to the physical world. The main problem can be stated as follows: is time a fundamental substance, capable of independent existence, or is it ontologically dependent on things (events)? One particular way of cashing out this question is by asking whether it is possible for time to exist without any change. Imagine the following situation: the entire universe suddenly freezes in its current state for one hundred years. Is such a possibility even intelligible? Can time keep ticking away even if no clock can do the actual ticking? Philosophers sympathetic to empiricism argue that if there is no way even in principle to observe or detect a certain phenomenon, we should refrain from postulating its existence. And clearly there is no way to observe a "total freeze", since the observers are in a frozen state as well. For all we know our own universe could be such that every minute it goes through a period of a static state with no change occurring. But this seems absurd. The requirement of economy, or parsimony, dictates that of two hypotheses which equally well account for observable data we should choose the one that is simpler. And the hypothesis which does not postulate any unobservable frozen periods in the history of the universe looks simpler than its rival.

Surprisingly, there is an ingenious argument due to Sidney Shoemaker showing that in some cases the requirement of simplicity can actually favor the hypothesis of periods of time without change. Suppose that the universe consists of three parts *A*, *B*, and *C*, and that the available empirical data show that each region undergoes a period of freeze in regular successions. That is, repeated observations confirm that region *A* freezes every three years, region *B* freezes every four years, and region *C* every five years. From these generalizations it follows that every sixty years all three regions should freeze simultaneously, but this obviously can't be confirmed empirically. But Shoemaker observes that the hypothesis assuming the possibility of a "total freeze" of the universe is much simpler than the alternative one which stipulates that the regular patterns of behavior of the three regions *A*, *B*, *C* will be broken every sixty years. Thus even the empiricist should prefer the hypothesis which implies that time without change is possible.

The question of the relation between time and the physical world can be spelled out in an even more radical way. We may ask whether it is possible for time to exist without any events taking place at all. Can there be periods of time consisting of empty moments, i.e. moments at which nothing exists at all? Those who believe that such a situation is fundamentally possible must assume that moments of time are entities whose existence is independent of the existence of events and things. This position in philosophy of time is called absolutism or substantivalism. The opposing view is referred to as relationism. Relationists believe that only physical objects in space and time (such as events or things) exist in the fundamental sense.

Temporal objects (moments) are derived from temporal relations that hold among physical objects. We have already seen how moments can be defined in this approach: they are taken to be sets of simultaneous events. Clearly, if there are no events, there can be no moments thus defined. It has to be noted that an analogous ontological problem concerns the nature of space. Absolutism with respect to space amounts to the claim that space is an independent substance existing regardless of the objects occupying it. Relationists, on the other hand, define space in terms of the relation of collocation: a point of space is a set of all events which are collocated with one another.

Historically, the controversy between absolutism and relativism began in earnest with the famous dispute between Gottfried Leibniz and Isaac Newton. Leibniz, the founding father of relationism, conceived of two arguments against substantivalism. The first one is known as the static shift argument. If space consists of points whose identity does not depend on what transpires in them, then there should be an ontological difference between the universe as it is now and a universe in which every single object is shifted 10 meters in a given direction. Because the same objects in both universes would occupy numerically different points, such a static shift would produce a new state of affairs. But it is absurd to expect that such two universes would differ at all. God could not have any reason to create the world in one place rather than in another. (This argument can be formulated for time as well: there can be no qualitative difference between our universe and an identical universe which started five minutes earlier.) The kinematic shift argument, on the other hand, compares the following two scenarios: a stationary universe, and a universe which moves uniformly in a selected direction. If space is absolute, these two universes differ with respect to their motion relative to spatial points. And yet there is no way to tell which universe we actually occupy. Moreover, the existence of such indistinguishable and yet distinct universes would clearly violate the Principle of the Identity of Indiscernibles.

There is an interesting albeit subtle difference between the two arguments presented by Leibniz (this difference was brought to the surface by Tim Maudlin). The static shift argument begins with reference to our universe and its location in absolute space. Once we introduce the term "the point at which the mass center of the universe is located" we can consider a possible world in which the center of the universe is located ten meters away from this point (observe that the expression in quotes has to be considered a rigid designator). But the kinematic shift example can be introduced without reference to the actual universe. The stationary universe is defined as a universe whose location in absolute space does not change in time, whereas a moving universe occupies different spatial locations at different moments. Consequently, in the second example it may be correctly claimed that there is no way for us to tell whether our universe is stationary or moving. However, in the first case it is quite trivial to observe that by assumption our universe is the original one, and not the shifted one. Thus it is inappropriate to say (as some do) that we can't know which of the two possible worlds we inhabit. But Leibniz's point still stands that there is no qualitative difference between the two worlds considered in the static case. We know that our world is the initial one not because it differs qualitatively from the shifted one, but because we designated the initial world to be identical with ours.

Newton met the challenge created by Leibniz's kinematic shift example head-on by showing that in some special cases the difference between a static and a moving universe can be actually observed. But this applies only to accelerated motions, such as rotations. Newton's famous argument in support of his absolutism is known as the bucket argument. Consider a bucket full of water suspended on a rope. When we twist the rope and then let go, initially the bucket will rotate but the water will remain stationary for a while. Later on, as the water catches up with the sides of the bucket, it too starts to rotate, and this causes its surface to become concave due to the centrifugal force. Finally we stop the bucket, but the water is still twirling, and the surface remains concave. When we compare the first and third stages of the experiment we can note that they do not differ with respect to the relative motion of the bucket and water. But there is an observable difference in the behavior of the water: in the first stage its surface is flat, but in the third stage it is curved. Newton explains this by saying that only in the third stage does the water "really" rotate – that is, it rotates with respect to absolute space. Accelerated motions with respect to absolute space create inertial forces (so-called g-forces), and this shows that absolute space exists.

The Austrian physicist and philosopher Ernest Mach was not convinced by Newton's argument. He pointed out that the situation

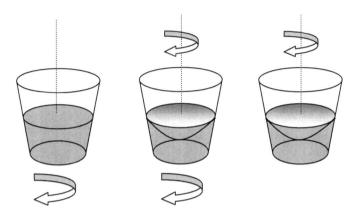

Three stages of Newton's bucket experiment.

in which the bucket rotates and the water is stationary is not exactly symmetrical with respect to the later phase in which the bucket stops and the water keeps rotating. Newton ignored one important element of the experiment: the existence of the remaining objects in the universe (including the Earth and other celestial bodies). Newton's argument would be valid if in the first stage of the experiment we somehow managed to make the entire universe, including the bucket, spin around the stationary water. But obviously this can't be done, so it is a mere speculation to assume that in this case the surface of the water would remain flat. Mach's criticism is sometimes interpreted as suggesting the hypothesis that all inertial forces are a result of the influence of the remaining masses of the universe. But Mach only wanted to say that we can't make any definitive claims as to the result of the bucket experiment when properly conducted.

Mach's ideas were further developed by Albert Einstein in his general theory of relativity (GTR). Einstein was dissatisfied with the fact that the special theory of relativity differentiated between inertial and non-inertial (i.e. accelerated) frames of reference. The laws of special relativity are the same in all inertial frames, but this is not the case for non-inertial ones. A new theory should make all frames of reference fundamentally equivalent, and therefore should realize the relationist's dream of dispensing altogether with absolute motions, whether accelerated or not. This ideal was supposed to be achieved in the general theory of relativity. Einstein postulated it to be generally covariant, which means that its laws should remain unchanged under any "smooth" transformation of coordinates. Accelerating frames of reference are equivalent to inertial frames in a gravitational field. Einstein's field equation, which is the core of general relativity, connects the distribution of mass and energy with the geometrical property of space-time, known as its curvature. Space-time is no longer flat (Euclidean), but has a structure of semi-Riemannian geometry with variable curvature.

Returning to the issue of how GTR dispenses with the notion of absolute motion (acceleration), we have to note that the situation is far from being clear. Thanks to the Equivalence Principle (which effectively asserts that gravitational mass and inertial mass are identical) an accelerated frame of reference (such as a space rocket) is empirically indistinguishable from the same frame at rest in a uniform gravitational field. This gravitational field may be assumed to be produced by the remaining masses of the universe accelerating with respect to the chosen frame. But the equations of GTR admit a situation in which there is no matter in the universe other than a test body. In this case the inertial forces produced by the acceleration of this body cannot be explained as coming from distant objects, since there are no distant objects to produce any gravitational field. Moreover, the field equation of GTR admits yet another troublesome solution in which the universe contains no body except for a single, rotating object. But the relationist cannot accept the notion of rotation if there is no other body that this rotation can be relative to. In conclusion, the controversy between absolutism and relationism is far from being resolved even in light of the most recent developments in physics.

Time's arrow and time travel

In the next step we will consider the question of the objectivity of time's direction, or time's arrow as it is sometimes called. The directionality of time seems to follow from the fact that temporal points are ordered by the earlier-than relation. But spatial points can be also put in order with the help of a specially prepared relation. We have already seen that points on a meridian can be ordered with respect to their closeness to the North Pole or the South Pole. Is there any difference between the temporal ordering of moments and the spatial ordering of points? Formally, the two orderings are on a par. But it may be observed that the difference between the two lies in the fact that the ordering of spatial points requires an external "point of reference", whereas the earlier-than relation which orders temporal points is not relative to any such fixed point. Those who believe in the objective character of time's directionality would probably agree that the relation of being earlier than connecting two moments is an intrinsic relation which does not depend on anything external from those moments. But an analogous ordering relation applied to spatial points is always given with respect to some other points, and those reference points are selected in a rather arbitrary fashion.

Assuming the objective character of the directionality of time, we may nevertheless ask the question whether it is a primitive feature of time, or can it be grounded in some more fundamental properties. There are three basic suggestions as to what can ground time's arrow: it may be the psychological arrow, the causal arrow, and the thermodynamic arrow. The concept of the psychological arrow is based on the observation that perceptions always precede memories. My perception of a given occurrence is designated as happening earlier than my memory of the same occurrence. Although this criterion of temporal precedence can be directly applied to mental events only, by extension it can be projected onto other events, provided that they can be temporarily correlated with our mental states. But the idea of grounding time's directionality in the psychological arrow has obvious shortcomings. To begin with, memories are notoriously unreliable. People often claim to have recollections of events that have never actually taken place. Moreover, the psychological criterion excludes from the outset the metaphysical possibility of having "memories" of the future (they can be more appropriately called "precognitions"). If I had had a clear vision of an asteroid hitting London, and then the actual catastrophe took place exactly as seen by me, based on the aforementioned criterion I would have to admit that my vision occurred later than the actual hitting. On top of that, the psychological arrow is obviously anthropocentric, as it presupposes that without humans (or any sentient beings whose psychology is similar to ours) there would be no succession of events. But this is hard to believe, unless we assume some form of idealism (the thesis of the dependence of reality on perceptions).

Some philosophers point out that there is a deeper reason why perceptions occur earlier than their memories. This is so, because perceptions are causes of subsequent memories. The hypothesis of the causal arrow reduces the temporal order to the more fundamental causal one. Thus it is assumed that if event x causes another event y, x has to be earlier than y. The causal explication of time's arrow rejects the subjective character of the direction of time, and this is a step in the right direction. However, some problems persist in this approach. First of all, the causal relation itself has to be characterized in a way that does not explicitly presuppose the temporal succession of cause and effect. As we will see in the next chapter, the regularity conception of causality does just that – it assumes from the outset that causation amounts to a type of temporal succession of events. For that reason this conception of causation is unsuitable for the task of explaining the temporal order, and alternative conceptions need to be considered. Another complication is that we have to exclude the possibility of non-standard causal links which go backward in time. Even though there are no indications that such causal link exist, some philosophers insist that they are not in principle impossible (for instance the idea of time travel directly involves such backward links, as we will soon see).

The most popular way to ground time's arrow is based on the physical theory of thermodynamics. It is well known that certain processes in nature are irreversible, i.e. they occur in one direction only (for instance the processes of heat transfer or mixing). Irreversible processes are always associated with a change of the physical quantity known as entropy, which measures the degree of disorder of a system. Those processes lead from a state which is more ordered to a state which is less ordered (and thus from lower entropy to higher entropy). The second law of thermodynamics states that in an isolated system (a system which does not exchange energy with its environment) the entropy never decreases (it increases until the system reaches the state called an equilibrium in which the entropy remains constant). The thermodynamic arrow of time is expressed in a stipulation which designates the states of an isolated system with lower entropy as earlier from the states of greater entropy. The main problem affecting the second law is that it seems to be inconsistent with the full time-reversibility of the underlying laws of Newtonian mechanics. A famous attempt to resolve this situation was made by Ludwig Boltzmann, an Austrian physicist. His reduction of thermodynamics to statistical mechanics is based on the distinction between macrostates, defined with the help of macroscopic parameters such as temperature, pressure, etc., and microstates, given by specifying the positions and velocities of all molecules. Each macrostate can be realized by a number of different microstates. Boltzmann proved that for a given macrostate the overwhelming majority of corresponding microstates are such that their dynamic evolution leads to the increase of entropy. This result is commonly interpreted as confirming the second law as a highly probable rule of macroscopic evolution.

However, there is one important problem with Boltzmann's argument. Due to the reversibility of the underlying dynamics, his argument can be turned around to show that for a given macrostate it is also overwhelmingly probable that it has evolved from a state of even higher entropy, which contradicts observed facts. In order to account for the observable thermodynamic asymmetry, it is usually assumed that Boltzmann's argument has to be augmented by an additional premise about the initial state of the universe. The so-called low entropy hypothesis states that the universe started its evolution in a state with an extremely low value of entropy, and therefore the highly probable path of its evolution led in the direction of increasing entropy.

Time travel has been the topic of many science-fiction stories, but it has also attracted a lot of attention from scientists and philosophers. In metaphysics we are primarily interested in the question of the conceptual possibility of traveling in time. Some believe that time travel is ultimately inconsistent and therefore impossible. Others reply that the apparent inconsistencies are mere oddities and that they don't make time travel fundamentally impossible. The first step of our analysis should be a clarification of what time travel is. The proposed definition is based on the distinction between the internal time of an observer and the external time related to the environment. The internal time of a person is determined by the usual physical and psychological processes, such as metabolism, ageing, perceptions and memories. Time travel occurs when the internal time of the observer differs from the external time. It is worth noting that this definition implies that one particular type of time travel is admissible in special relativity, due to the effect known as time dilation. As is well known, the duration of a process concerning an object which moves with respect to our frame is longer than the duration of the same process measured internally. Thus if an observer sets out on a high-speed journey and then comes back to the starting point, his internal time will show a shorter duration of the trip than the external clocks. This means that the observer has essentially travelled into the future. But the most intriguing type of time travel is when the departure point as measured by external time is later than the moment of arrival. This is what we call travel into the past.

One argument against the possibility of traveling into the past is based on the assumption that the past cannot be changed. Suppose that the traveler journeys a hundred years back in time and leaves a mark there – for instance makes an inscription on a rock. It may be argued that the traveler actually changed the past, because before his journey the inscription on the rock was not yet done, hence the rock must have been clear. But this argument commits an error of confusing two temporal orders: the external and the internal ones. With respect to the internal time the act of inscription is located in the future, but with respect to the external time it is in the past. There are no two states of affairs inconsistent with one another (the inscribed rock and the rock with no inscription on it). There are only two ways to temporally relate the act of inscription with a particular moment just before the journey.

But the critics can consider a particular troublesome type of action that apparently can be performed in the past. What if the traveler interferes in the past with the causal process that subsequently led to the journey itself or even his very existence? This is the basis of the famous grandfather paradox in which the traveler goes back in time, kills his grandfather and therefore prevents himself from being born. This scenario is an example of a vicious causal loop: an event A causes an event B in the past, but B prevents A from occurring. Clearly such a situation cannot take place. But what is to stop the time traveler from carrying out his evil plan of doing in his grandpa? David Lewis believes that the problem is caused by the equivocal character of the word "can". In one sense the traveler can kill his grandfather, but in another he can't. Relative to the set of facts which include only certain qualities of the traveler and his immediate surroundings (his ability to go through with his plan, his determination, the immediate circumstances of the ambush, etc.) he can kill the grandfather. But relative to the fact that the grandfather lived to have children and grandchildren, he can't. However, Lewis's solution does not explain the objective and potentially empirically verifiable fact that all attempts to kill the grandfather in the past are bound to fail. This is clearly different from ordinary actions involving forward-looking causal links. Although in some cases a particular plot to assassinate a given person may fail, statistically there is a significant rate of success. Thus if backward causal links exist, they must be extremely sensitive to external conditions. Each time when a supposed causal correlation can result in a vicious loop, the correlation must be destroyed to prevent a contradiction.

How things exist in time

The last topic considered in this chapter will be the metaphysical analysis of the way things exist in time (this type of existence is also referred to as persistence). The crucial fact about persistence is that each persisting thing remains the same object (in a suitable sense of the word "same") throughout its existence. A tree may grow taller and denser, but it still remains the same tree. The relation that holds between a thing at one time and the same thing at another time is called diachronic identity (or genetic identity – genidentity for short). One of the most important questions about diachronic identity is whether it is related to (or perhaps even coincides with) numerical identity, or is it an entirely new type of identity. This question is answered differently by two major competing theories of persistence, known as endurantism and perdurantism. Endurantism can be characterized broadly as the position according to which things persist by being wholly and completely present at every single moment of their existence (we call this type of persistence endurance). Endurantism seems to be in agreement with our pre-philosophical intuitions regarding persistence. When I take a look at a desk in front of me, I believe that no part of the desk is missing at this very moment. Next day I will again look at a complete desk, even if some of its properties are slightly different (for instance its top is a bit dustier). In accordance with common sense endurantism assumes that things can only have spatial parts, and therefore they are three-dimensional spatial objects that exist at different moments. Regarding the question of diachronic identity, the answer supplied by endurantism is simple: diachronic identity is just the numerical identity of an object with itself. The expressions "Napoleon at the

Battle of Austerlitz" and "Napoleon at the Battle of Waterloo" refer to one and the same individual: Napoleon.

Perdurantism, on the other hand, departs from common sense by assuming that things are actually four-dimensional objects, where the fourth dimension is the temporal one. My desk extends in time as well as in space, and at each moment I can see only one fragment of the entire object, whereas the remaining fragments consist of past and future stages of the desk. More specifically, what we usually identify as things perceived by us are not full objects but their three-dimensional slices. It is also possible to speak about temporal stages of things, where a stage of a thing x is a part of x which occupies a non-zero temporal interval. Consequently, the descriptions "Napoleon at the Battle of Austerlitz" and "Napoleon at the Battle of Waterloo" refer to two numerically distinct objects: two slices (or stages) of the four-dimensional entity that we call "Napoleon". Thus according to perdurantism the relation of diachronic identity is not reducible to numerical identity. Instead, it can be defined as the relation of being different slices of the same four-dimensional object. It is noteworthy to observe that the way things persist according to perdurantism (in short, the way things perdure) is analogous to the temporal way of existence for events. As we stressed earlier, events are never fully present at intervals shorter than their entire duration.

What may be the reason to prefer such a contrived position as perdurantism to the more natural endurantism? The main motivation for perdurantism comes from the problem of change which afflicts the endurantist approach. When a thing changes in time, it possesses a particular property P at one moment t, and ceases to possess P at another moment t'. But if the things existing at both times are numerically identical, then we have a contradiction: one and the same thing possesses P and doesn't possess P. Perdurantism solves this problem neatly by attributing each of the contradictory properties P and non-P to numerically distinct objects: two different temporal slices of the same four-dimensional entity. But endurantism is not without options either. One possible solution is to accept that properties are always relative to time. A poker which is hot at moment t and cold at t' does not possess the mutually inconsistent properties of being hot and being cold, but rather the properties of being-hot-at-moment-t and being-cold-at-moment-t', and these properties do not exclude one another as long as t is different from t'. But some philosophers object to the idea that all properties should be indexed by time. They observe that this implies that all properties turn out to be fundamentally relational, as they connect things and instants of time. An alternative option is to relativize not the properties themselves but the relation of possession (exemplification). Thus we would have to admit that there are not one but infinitely many relations of exemplification indexed by temporal instances (exemplification at moment t, exemplification at t', and so on).

There is, however, a more sophisticated argument against endurantism that requires closer scrutiny. This argument is due to Peter van Inwagen, with some corrections added by Mark Heller. Suppose that a person X undergoes an amputation of his left hand. Let t_1 denote a moment before, and t_2 a moment after the amputation. Let us also denote by "X-minus" the whole consisting of X's body without the left hand (regardless of whether the hand is attached to or separated from it). It seems that the endurantist should accept the following three identities:

(1) X at $t_1 = X$ at t_2
(2) X-minus at $t_1 = X$-minus at t_2
(3) X-minus at $t_2 = X$ at t_2.

However, from these premises we can derive, using only the assumption of the transitivity of identity, that

(4) X at $t_1 = X$-minus at t_1

This conclusion is clearly unacceptable. The body of a person who is not missing any hands is not identical with the body minus the left hand. In order to see what could have possibly gone wrong with the argument, let us review the justification that the endurantist can offer in support of the premises (1)-(3). Premise (1) follows from the endurantist's claim that diachronic identity is numerical identity, plus the additional assumption that losing one's hand does not imply losing one's identity. Premise (2) is a simple consequence of endurantism. And premise (3) is supported by the principle according to which two numerically distinct things cannot occupy the same spatial region at the same time. Now it should be clear how the perdurantist can block the way to the unwanted conclusion (4). If we agree that the expressions "X at t_1 (t_2)" and "X-minus at t_1 (t_2)" refer

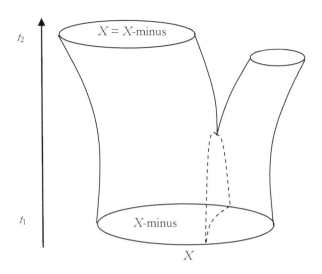

t_2

$X = X\text{-minus}$

t_1

$X\text{-minus}$

X

The amputation case

to temporal slices of appropriate four-dimensional objects, premises (1) and (2) become evidently false (no two slices taken at different moments can be numerically identical). On the other hand, if we interpret these expressions as referring to whole four-dimensional objects (for instance when we point at Napoleon at the moment of the Battle of Waterloo we may want to refer to the whole Napoleon, and not his temporal stage), then premises (1)-(2) are true, but now the third premise is false (two distinct four-dimensional objects can nevertheless share some temporal slices).

But the endurantist has some strategies of defense available – actually as many as four. Firstly, she can insist that the person after the amputation is not identical with the person before it. The loss of a hand is sufficient to create a new person. But this sounds very unconvincing. Observe that the same paradox can be recreated even when we consider a minute and seemingly insignificant loss of parts, such as clipping a fingernail. It is rather desperate to admit that after clipping one's fingernails or trimming one's hair a new person is born. Perhaps a slightly better response from the endurantist would be to argue that both premise (1) and conclusion (4) are affected by the same degree of vagueness. That is, if we limit ourselves to the types of part losses which are so minuscule that they make (1) look true, by the same token we should accept (4) within a reasonable margin of error (a body and a body minus one hair are roughly identical). On the other hand, if the considered part loss is sufficiently big to make (4) false, (1) should be deemed false as well. But intuitively it doesn't look like (1) and (4) stand and fall together. Common sense dictates that if the loss of parts is extended over a long period of time, it may gradually accumulate to a large percentage of the initial volume without any loss of identity. But this is not the case with the synchronic identity (taken at the same moment).

In the second strategy the existence of the object named *X-minus* is called into question. For instance van Inwagen rejects the position he calls the doctrine of the existence of arbitrary and undetached parts. *X-minus* before the amputation is not a separate, autonomous object (an organism, for instance), but an undetached and rather arbitrarily selected part of the entire human body, and therefore its existence can be doubted. But this solution has the unintuitive consequence that in some cases objects which are not simples can nevertheless lack any proper parts. If we take a functioning organism which cannot be separated into any autonomous and relatively isolated parts, we have to admit that this organism has no proper parts. But clearly an organism is not a simple atom.

The most promising strategy for the endurantist, in my opinion, is to deny the principle that two distinct things never occupy precisely the same spatial region. This principle derives its initial appeal from the so-called impenetrability assumption which seems to be applicable to physical objects. But the impenetrability assumption states only that if you have two things which at a certain moment are fully separated in space, they cannot later overlap spatially, i.e. occupy the same region of space at the same time. However, it may still be claimed that there are distinct things which always overlap during the period of their common existence. Consider for instance the following example: a lump of clay and a statue made of this clay. It may be argued that throughout the entire existence of the statue it occupies precisely the same spatial location as the lump of clay. But the lump of clay and the statue are not numerically identical, since the lump existed before the creation of the statue, and it will presumably exist after the destruction of the statue. The lump and the statue have different conditions of survival, and hence are different objects, even if they happen to coincide spatiotemporally. If we agree with this argument, we can reasonably question premise (3). X and X-minus are not numerically identical, even though at some moments they coincide spatially, since at other moments (i.e. before the amputation) they clearly occupy non-identical regions (X-minus is a proper part of X at t_1).

There is yet another strategy considered by some defenders of endurantism, which rejects the assumption of the transitivity of numerical identity. This move is based on a rather idiosyncratic conception of identity proposed by Peter Thomas Geach, according to which identity statements should always be relativized to a particular general category. Thus we shouldn't say that x is the same as y, but rather that x is the same person as y, or x is the same body as y, or x is the same universal as y, etc. In our example premise (1) should be interpreted as stating that X at t_1 is the same person as X at t_2, whereas premise (3) ought to be read as "X at t_2 is the same body as X-minus at t_2". From these premises it neither follows that X at t_1 is the same person as X-minus at t_2, nor that they are the same bodies. But it seems that the same paradox can be repeated using an unambiguous concept of identity with respect to one particular category (for instance identity interpreted as being the same body). It still makes intuitive sense to claim that my car at one moment is the same body as my car at a later time with one screw removed, and of course my car minus the screw and my car are the same bodies after the removal. Thus this strategy offers little help for the endurantist.

5 CAUSATION

Our physical universe consists of bodies which are mutually connected by a web of various relations. First and foremost, there are spatiotemporal relations that determine the relative locations of things in space and time. We have also discussed how objects can be related to each other with respect to their common properties (as expressed in various degrees of similarity and qualitative identity). But the list of fundamental metaphysical relations would be woefully incomplete without the causal relation. Causality is appropriately called the cement of the universe. Causal interactions between physical bodies help to combine them into larger structures: molecules, cells, organisms, planetary systems, galaxies, etc. Virtually everything that happens around us is brought about by causation. Earthquakes cause damage, sunlight causes photosynthesis, and stock market collapses cause panic. But what does it mean that something causes something else? As usual, we will start off with some basic distinctions. To begin with, we should differentiate between general causal statements, such as "Smoking causes cancer", and singular causal statements of the type "The sinking of the Titanic was caused by a collision with an iceberg". General causal statements involve types of events, whereas singular statements concern individual occurrences. There are no simple logical rules connecting the two types of causal statements. For instance, it would be inappropriate to infer from the statement that smoking causes cancer that each individual who smokes more than a given number of cigarettes a day will develop cancer. On the other hand, there is no easy method of generalizing singular causal statements in order to reveal the underlying causal link between types of events. This is the case, because for a given event there is usually more than one way of categorizing it into a broader type. For instance, an individual act of smoking a cigarette can be subsumed under the category of inhaling the chemicals produced in the process of burning tobacco leaves, but also under the category of being engaged in a nerve-soothing practice, or moving particular muscles of the mouth and the chest. Only the first categorization leads to causal generalizations involving serious health issues.

In what follows we will focus almost exclusively on singular causal statements. Hence we will interpret causation, as it is commonly done, to be a relation between individual objects. But what objects can be properly taken as causes and effects? One suggestion may be that causes are things which make something happen. In everyday speech we say for instance that a stone shattered the window, or that an asteroid wiped out the dinosaurs. But when we look closer we can see that this is a very imprecise way of speaking. A stone that is lying on the ground does not cause any shattering, and an asteroid which stays on its orbit at a safe distance from Earth does not threaten life on our planet. Strictly speaking, it is not things that cause something to happen, but what these things are doing. The dinosaurs went extinct because of the hit of an asteroid, which was an event. Thus it is natural to assume that both causes and effects are events involving certain things, not things themselves. But some philosophers suggest that this account of causality is too restrictive, as it doesn't make room for cases of what can be called negative causation. Sometimes it seems natural to single out the absence of an event rather than an event itself as a cause of a particular occurrence. We say that the lack of attention of the driver was a cause of the crash, and the absence of working sprinklers causally contributed to the fire. In order to admit negative causation (sometimes also called causation by omission) some propose to interpret causes and effects as facts, not events. Facts are objective counterparts of true statements, so if a statement about the absence of an event is true, there is a fact corresponding to this statement. But it is not entirely clear whether we really need negative causation. It may be pointed out that underlying any case of negative causation there is an even more fundamental instance of positive causation –

for example the lack of attention of the driver could have been actually due to his talking on his mobile. Moreover, some examples of causation by omission are clearly unintuitive. For instance we wouldn't normally accept the statement "The fact that I was not struck by lightning caused me to survive" unless we had a reason to believe that the lightning was imminent.

Let's continue our analysis of the causal relation connecting events, and let's focus on some of its basic formal features. It should be relatively clear that causation is not reflexive (my typing of this sentence certainly doesn't cause itself). But is it irreflexive? In other words, can there be special events which are their own causes? That depends on some additional assumptions. If we allow causal loops, which can occur for instance in time travel (we have discussed this in Chapter 4), and if we accept that the causal relation is transitive, then it follows that one event can be its own cause. This can happen when event x causes event y in the past, but y causes x in turn. This situation is of course only hypothetical, as we don't have any evidence for the existence of backward causal links, but some philosophers insist that there is nothing fundamentally incoherent about this possibility. The possibility of causal loops also shows that the causal relation is not necessarily asymmetric, although clearly in the overwhelming majority of cases if x causes y, y doesn't cause x (thus causality is certainly not symmetric). As for transitivity, it is usually assumed that causation is transitive: if one event x causes event y, and y in turn causes another event z, we naturally expect x to be a causal factor in creating z as well. But recently several cases have been considered which seem to undermine this conclusion. Consider, for instance, the following scenario: a bomb had been planted at a politician's office before it was spotted by the security service and disarmed. We should agree that the planting of the bomb caused its disarming, and the disarming in turn causally secured the politician's survival. But it sounds a bit odd to admit that the planting of the bomb was causally responsible for the survival of the politician. Still, this situation is far from clear, as some philosophers (including Lewis) insist that there is nothing wrong with the last statement – it only shows that sometimes actual consequences of our actions are different from the intended ones. Thus the issue of the transitivity of the causal relation remains contentious.

Regularity analysis of causation

But what exactly is causal relation? All modern debates regarding this question are heavily indebted to David Hume and his critical analysis of causation. Hume observed first that it seems incontrovertible that all cases of causation display the following two features: spatio-temporal contiguity and temporal succession. That is, if an event x is a cause of an event y, x and y have to be contiguous (they have to "touch" each other spatiotemporally), and moreover x has to be earlier than y. For instance, if a stone flies towards a window pane and shatters the glass, we can clearly observe that the cause (the flight of the stone) and the effect (the shattering of the glass) literally touch each other in space and time, and of course the effect comes about a moment later after the cause. Incidentally, both characteristics of causation given by Hume can be actually questioned, and for a good reason. In the age of cell phones we know very well that a cause (for instance my dialing a number) does not have to be close in space to its effect (the ringing of my friend's phone). It may be replied that Hume most probably had in mind direct causes and effects. In the phone connection example my dialing is just the first in a series of events involving an electromagnetic signal leaving my phone and getting to the receiving phone, so it may be claimed that the requirement of contiguity is still satisfied. However, there is nothing inconsistent in the idea of an action at a distance, in which the cause and effect are not connected by any chain of intermediate events. For instance, in Newtonian mechanics gravity is assumed to propagate exactly in such a non-local way through space. As for the requirement of temporal succession, we have already observed in the previous chapter that the idea of causal links going backward in time is not self-contradictory. Hence it doesn't look like the two conditions introduced by Hume are indeed necessary for causation.

But Hume notices that they are not sufficient either. There are numerous cases of pairs of events mutually contiguous in space and occurring in succession which are nevertheless not connected causally. If I touch a random key on my cell phone and immediately after that the phone rings, this is just a coincidence, not a causal link. Some philosophers (mostly before Hume) insisted that there has to be a necessary connection between any two events which are causally linked. The shattering of the glass not only just follows the hitting by the stone – it follows with necessity. Given the circumstances, the glass has to shatter. But Hume eloquently argued that there is no logical necessity in the occurrence of the effect after the cause. I can imagine without contradiction that the stone magically passes through the glass, or bounces off it. And no idea of necessary link is present in our perception of events. All we can see is a conjunction of two occurrences. The only extra element that can be derived from experience is the idea of constancy or repetition. We believe that the shattering follows necessarily the hitting, because we have seen numerous times that stones flying into glass panes shatter them. Thus we have been conditioned to expect the effect after its cause. But objectively there is only the constant conjunction of two independent events, and that's that.

The conception of causality which arises as a result of Hume's critical analysis is known as the regularity account. In Hume's version of this approach an event x is a cause of an event y, if x is spatiotemporally contiguous with y, x temporally precedes y, and every event similar to x is followed by an event similar to y. An immediate problem with this characterization is that the notion of similarity is fatally vague and context-dependent. To avoid this difficulty we may want to start not with individual events but with their broad categories. This is actually what we do in everyday practice – in our earlier example we have already categorized the considered events involving the stone and the window by describing them as hitting and shattering respectively. But this would mean that prior to the analysis of individual cases of causation we would have to start with an explanation of general causal statements. Even if we manage to clear this first obstacle, there are more problems with the Humean analysis. It is commonly accepted that Hume's definition of causality is both too broad and too narrow; that is it lets in cases which are not causal, but excludes some other unquestionable cases. Critics point out that persistent but accidental regularities may satisfy Hume's definition without being causal. Days regularly follow nights, and yet there is no causal connection between them. Similarly, if according to the train timetable one train always arrives at a given station right after the other one leaves, this does not mean that one event causes the other. It may be interesting to notice that in both cases the observed regularities can be explained not by a direct causal link but rather by the existence of a common cause of the two correlated events. In the case of the regular succession of days and nights the common cause is the rotation of the Earth, whereas in the second case it is the timetable regulating the arrivals and departures of trains. Thus Hume's version of the regularity theory has a problem with distinguishing direct causal links from links that arise as a consequence of a third factor.

Another group of counterexamples to Humean analysis contains cases of causal links without regular succession. In everyday life we often identify one event as a cause of another without implying that events of the same type as the selected cause always produce the required result. For instance we can agree that the failure of the brakes was a cause of a given car accident without accepting that each case of the same type of failure leads to a similar accident. The reason for this is that causal links are highly dependent on external conditions. The failure of brakes can produce a particular accident only when it occurs together with a number of other factors: when the car is speeding and another car is approaching, when the road bends sharply, etc. We may also express this thought by saying that there are many causal factors leading to a given effect, and only if we take all of them into account we may suggest that there is a regular succession. Some philosophers also point out that there may be unique events in the history of the universe which nevertheless are connected causally. For instance the Big Bang was a one-off event, and yet it is uncontroversial that it did cause a lot of things, including the fact that we are here now discussing the issue of causality. But events which are not repeatable cannot be tested for their causal connections by the regularity approach.

Attempts to remedy some of these problems are made in modern neo-Humean regularity approaches. As an example we will discuss the so-called nomological approach to causation. According to it, an event x of type A is considered a cause of an event y of type B in conditions C, if there is a law of nature L such that L together with the sentence that an event of type A occurred in conditions C logically imply that an event of type B will happen. To illustrate: my pressing the button causes the light bulb to flash under the condition that the electric circuit is unbroken and connected to the mains, because according to the appropriate laws of physics in a closed circuit the current will pass through the filament of the light bulb and the filament will get hot and start giving off light. The reference to laws in the nomological approach is supposed to eliminate instances of accidental regularities, while the introduction of background conditions C stresses the fact that the observed regularities are strongly context-dependent (they may not occur in different conditions). In spite of correcting the main shortcomings of Hume's original version of the regularity approach, the nomological theory suffers from new ailments. First of all, the notion of a law of nature is notoriously difficult to explicate. One possible account of laws, advocated by Hume himself, reduces them to mere regularities. But this means that the concept of causation based on laws will ultimately come down to Hume's original regularity notion with all its flaws. Some philosophers insist that laws have to contain an element of necessity which goes beyond mere generalizations or regularities. But then Hume's challenge returns in full force: how can we account for the necessity of laws if we can't observe it in experience? Some steps towards achieving this goal can be taken with the help of the modal semantics of possible worlds that we introduced in Chapter 3. But philosophers remain deeply divided on the issue of the necessary character of laws.

Another problem with the nomological approach is related to the fact that not all laws of nature are causal in nature – some of them instead describe the coexistence of certain phenomena. Consider for instance Pascal's law of hydrostatics which asserts that a sample of gas or liquid in a container exerts equal pressure on its walls in all directions. It follows from this law that we can derive the pressure exerted on one side of the container from the pressure applied to the other side, but this doesn't mean that one is a cause of the other. Rather, we are dealing here yet again with a case of a common cause. The pressure propagating in all directions is caused by one factor – the incessant motion of the molecules which is fundamentally random and therefore does not privilege any particular direction. A similar problem is connected with the fact that most laws of nature are time-reversible. Thus it is possible to derive an earlier state of a system from a later one using a particular law, but we can't deduce from this that the earlier state is caused by the later one. For instance, from the current position of the bodies in the solar system we can derive, using the laws of Newtonian mechanics, not only their future trajectories but the past ones as well. Yet we don't see this fact as an argument for the existence of backward causation.

INUS conditions and causality

One of the most sophisticated accounts of causation related to the regularity approach but in some respects transcending its limitations has been developed by John Mackie. Mackie's conception is based on two commonly used notions of sufficient and necessary conditions. Typically we characterize these notions as follows. C is a sufficient condition for an occurrence D, if each time when C holds, D happens. C is a necessary condition for D, if each time when D happens, C occurs as well (or, equivalently, if C does not hold, D doesn't happen). As it turns out, these definitions are in some respects problematic, and we will have to return to their proper analysis later. But for now let us accept them as they stand. Mackie notes first that causes are rarely, if ever, simply sufficient or necessary conditions for their effects. Consider the following example: a fire broke out in a house due to faulty wiring and consequently a short circuit. The short circuit itself is not sufficient for the fire to spread, for some other conditions have to hold, such as the presence of flammable materials and oxygen, the absence of automatic sprinklers or smoke detectors, and so on. On the other hand, the short circuit is not a necessary condition either, for the fire might have started in many different alternative ways (as a result of a lightning strike, or of a carelessly tossed cigarette butt, etc.). But Mackie observes that in the actual conditions which obtained before the fire the short circuit was in a sense necessary, for if we left everything else unchanged and took away the short circuit, no fire would ensue.

In order to make this intuition more precise, Mackie introduces the key notion of an INUS condition. INUS is an acronym that stands for "Insufficient but Necessary part of an Unnecessary but Sufficient condition". Let us try to disentangle this slightly convoluted concept using our fire example. Mackie believes that in this case the sum of all relevant conditions, including the short circuit, the presence of flammable materials, the lack of safety devices, etc., constitutes a sufficient condition for the occurrence of fire. But this whole sufficient condition is not necessary in the sense that there are many alternative conditions which would result in a similar fire. On the other hand, the short circuit is a necessary part of this actual sufficient condition, because without it the remaining conditions would not suffice for the fire to start. All this can be summarized in the following definition: A is an INUS condition for an event B, if there are conditions X and Y such that A together with X are a sufficient condition for B, but neither A nor X are by themselves sufficient conditions for B, and the disjunction AX or Y is sufficient and necessary for the occurrence of B. The symbol Y stands for the disjunction of all alternative conditions that might have sufficed for the fire. Additionally, Mackie requires that the conditions Y do not contain A as their necessary parts. An INUS condition for a given occurrence is by stipulation considered its cause, although Mackie admits that sometimes we may simply identify a whole sufficient or necessary condition as causally responsible for the effect. But INUS conditions constitute the most common types of causes.

In spite of its ingenuity, Mackie's definition of INUS condition admits some artificially created counterexamples, and therefore stands in need of some further corrections. To see this, let us use the letter C to abbreviate the sufficient condition for the fire as it happened, and let us consider an unrelated event S that by chance occurred simultaneously with C (for instance the fact that when the fire started somebody walked past the house whistling Beethoven's "Ode to joy"). It can be easily verified that the sentence "C or S and C or not-S" is logically equivalent to C, thus if there is a set of alternative conditions Y such that C and Y are jointly necessary and sufficient for the fire, the whole conjunction "$(C$ or S and C or not-$S)$ and Y" is also necessary and sufficient. But now we can observe that if we abbreviate "C or S" as A, and "C or not-S" as X, the above-stated definition of an INUS condition will be satisfied. Clearly neither C or S, nor C or not-S are sufficient for the fire (the whistling itself or its lack cannot produce a fire, and a disjunction is true if one of its disjuncts is true), but their conjunction is, as it is equivalent to C. But it is highly unintuitive to call the disjunctive event C or S a cause of the fire. Perhaps the additional requirement that causes cannot be disjunctions of events could help eliminate counterexamples of that type.

It should be clear that the conception of causation advocated by Mackie admits numerous distinct causes for one and the same event. Any element of the complex sufficient condition without which this condition would cease to be sufficient will do. Thus in our example the short circuit is an event satisfying the definition of an INUS condition, but so is the presence of oxygen, the low humidity of the air, and so forth. But we often prefer to pick one factor out of many as *the* cause of the event in question. Mackie observes that this choice is implicitly made relative to what he calls a causal field. A causal field contains all the conditions which we take for granted (as "normal"). If we for instance compare two virtually identical houses containing the same furniture, having the same fire safety systems (or a lack thereof), in the same weather conditions, such that one has gone up in flames whereas the other one has not, we can ask what difference between these houses can account for the fire. This means that we will take all the features shared by the two houses as belonging to the causal field, and we will call the relevant difference (for instance the fact that the burnt house had a short circuit) a cause of the fire. However, if we compare our house with a third one in which essentially the same type of short circuit happened but because of the installed automatic sprinklers the fire has been quickly extinguished, our verdict regarding the cause of the first fire will be different. Now the causal field contains the short circuit but not the lack of sprinklers, and only the latter fact will be deemed causally relevant. This point is so important (and yet so often ignored) that it may be worth repeating. The unqualified question "What caused event x?" is too unspecific to admit any useful answer (we may always truthfully but unhelpfully reply "The Big Bang caused it"). Instead, we should be asking questions of the sort "What is the causally relevant difference between the situation which led to event x, and an analogous situation which did not?". It is crucial to observe that the choice of the contrast situation limits possible answers to our question.

Now we should return to the definitions of necessary and sufficient conditions that we briefly mentioned at the beginning of this section. Mackie notices one fundamental problem with the proposed characteristics. If symbols C and D are interpreted as singular names of individual events, then it follows that each two events actually occurring in succession are necessary and sufficient conditions of each other. This is the case, because individual events can happen only once – a different fire of the same type is nevertheless a new event. So if my phone rang after I had pressed a button on it, it is true that each time when this particular pressing occurred (i.e. only once), this particular ringing followed. But of course we would not normally claim that my pressing is a sufficient condition for the ringing. On the other hand, if we decide to construe the symbols in the respective definitions as general terms, the new conception of causality is threatened by the types of problems affecting the standard regularity approach. Mackie suggests an interesting solution to this difficulty, which constitutes an important step beyond the regularity orthodoxy. He namely proposes to define the notions of necessary and sufficient conditions using so-called non-material (or non-truth-functional) conditionals. For instance a necessary condition of D is an individual event C such that if C had not occurred, D would not have happened. In the next section we will see how this type of conditional (known as counterfactual, or subjunctive conditionals) differs from the usual conditionals.

Counterfactual analysis of causation

According to some philosophers, regularity is not the hallmark of causation. As we have seen, not all regular connections are causal in nature, and some unquestionably causal links are nevertheless not regular. David Lewis famously suggested that we follow an alternative approach which is based on counterfactuality rather than regularity. The simplest version of such an approach (which we may call the naive counterfactual analysis) is based on the assumption that for an individual event x to cause another event y it has to be the case that if x had not happened, y would not have taken place either (in that case y is called counterfactually dependent on x). But this characteristic of the causal link is most certainly inadequate. For instance, suppose that I shut the door by slamming it. Clearly, if I hadn't shut the door, I would not have slammed it, but the shutting did not cause the slamming. In this case the counterfactual connection between the two events comes from the fact that both are in fact identical (my shutting and slamming are one and the same event). Another counterexample may be as follows: suppose that I have written the word "causality" on a piece of paper. If I hadn't scribbled the letters "caus", I wouldn't have written the entire expression, but again it is hard to admit that the writing of the first four letters caused the entire word to be inscribed. This time the relation between the two events is such that one constitutes part of the other. In order to avoid similar problems we have to assume that counterfactual causality applies only to distinct and separated events (i.e. events which are neither identical with nor parts of one another).

The prospects of the counterfactual theory of causation depend on our grasp on the semantics of counterfactual conditional sentences. For a long time philosophers remained deeply suspicious about counterfactuals, because their truth conditions cannot be given in a simple way analogous to the way we characterize sentences built with connectives such as "and", "or", etc. If we take for example the conjunction of two sentences "P and Q", the truth of the entire sentence depends only on the truth of the component sentences P and Q. The conjunction is true if both conjuncts P and Q are true, and if at least one of them is false, the entire conjunction is false. For that reason conjunctive statements are called truth-functional. However, it can be easily verified that the counterfactual "If it were P, it would be Q" is not truth-functional. The fact that both P and Q are false does not determine whether the entire sentence is true or false. Compare the following two statements "If my car were made of wood, it would float" and "If my car were made of wood, it would fly". Even though all simple sentences involved in these examples are false (my car is not made of wood, nor does it have the capability of floating or flying), the first conditional is true but the second false. There is no way to calculate the truth value of a counterfactual conditional on the basis of the truth values of its components.

Considerable progress in our understanding of how counterfactual conditionals work has been recently made thanks to the concerted effort of many logicians and philosophers, most prominently David Lewis. Lewis's analysis of counterfactuals is done within the semantics of possible worlds which we have discussed in Chapter 3. Lewis adds one important element to the conceptual framework of possible worlds: a new relation of relative similarity, or closeness, with respect to the actual world. That is, we assume that we can compare possible worlds regarding their similarity to the actual world. Intuitively we should agree that a world in which humans have the ability to fly is less similar to our world than a world in which I woke up today a minute later than I actually did. Using this notion of comparative similarity we can characterize the truth conditions for counterfactuals as follows. The statement "If it were P, then it would be Q" is true, if Q is true in all possible worlds in which P is true (in short: P-worlds) and which are most similar to the actual world among all P-worlds. That is, in order to evaluate a conditional with a particular counterfactual antecedent P, we have to imagine a situation in which P occurs, and which otherwise is as close to the actual situation as possible. For instance, we consider the statement "If this brick were made of ice, it would float" true, because in a world in which indeed the brick contains frozen water, but all the remaining facts and laws of the actual world are the same, the brick will float. However, this is not true for all possible worlds. We can imagine distant worlds in which ice is denser than liquid water, and therefore our brick would still sink. But such worlds do not enter the evaluation of the conditional in question, for we limit ourselves to the closest of all possible P-worlds.

The way we have characterized counterfactual conditionals has interesting implications regarding some of their formal features which differentiate them from other types of conditionals. It is well-known that the material conditional "If P, then Q" (which is a truth-functional type of statements) has the following property: if we add a new condition to the antecedent (the first sentence) of a true conditional, the resulting conditional will remain true. For instance, it is true that if a given animal is a mammal, this animal is warm-blooded, and hence it must be true that if an animal is a mammal and is also a sea creature, it is still warm-blooded. This procedure is called strengthening of the antecedent. But the law of the strengthening of the antecedent does not apply to counterfactuals. To see this, consider the following example. It is most probably true that if someone pointed a hand gun at my chest at close range and fired it, I would be dead. But if the shot was made and I was wearing a bullet-proof vest, I would survive. Thus it is possible that the counterfactual "If it were P, it would be Q" is true, and yet a strengthened-antecedent counterfactual "If it were P and R, it would be Q" is false. The first of the two statements is evaluated by considering the closest P-worlds and checking them for the truth of Q. The truth of the second conditional, on the other hand, depends on what transpires in the closest P-and-R-worlds, and these may be different from the closest P-worlds. To illustrate: in our earlier example the closest P-worlds are worlds in which I am fired at, but the clothes I am wearing are the same as in the actual world. But the closest P-and-R-worlds are selected by the additional requirement that I am protected by a bullet-proof vest.

The aforementioned logical property of counterfactuals has an important consequence for the account of causation based on this type of conditional statements. It namely confirms the already acknowledged fact that causal links are strongly dependent on background conditions, and therefore are not reducible to simple regularities. Supposing it is true about two distinct events x and y that

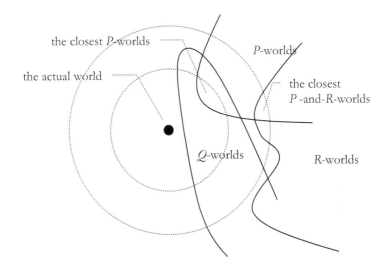

An illustration of the failure of the strengthening of the antecedent.
Points on the plane represent possible worlds. The closest P-worlds are
Q-worlds, but the closest P-and-R-worlds are not Q-worlds.

if x had not happened, y would not have happened (which means
that x is actually a cause of y), it still may be the case that if x had not
happened but some additional conditions obtained, y would have
occurred after all (and therefore in those conditions x would not be a
cause of y). This is what we should expect from a successful account
of causation. Another formal feature of counterfactuals relates to the
problem we have already mentioned at the beginning of this chapter,
namely the controversy surrounding the assumption of the
transitivity of the causal relation. It looks like the logic of
counterfactuals confirms the suspicion expressed by some
philosophers that causation may not be transitive after all. This is so,
because the relation of counterfactual dependence itself is not
transitive. It is possible to find three sentences P, Q, and R such that
it is true that if it were P, it would be Q, and if it were Q, it would be
R, but it is false that if it were P, it would be R. An example
illustrating this possibility has been already given – it is the case of a
failed bomb plot. It is true that if the bomb had not been planted, it
would not have been disarmed, and had it not been disarmed, the
politician would not have survived, but it is false that if the bomb had
not been planted, the politician would not have survived. Again, this

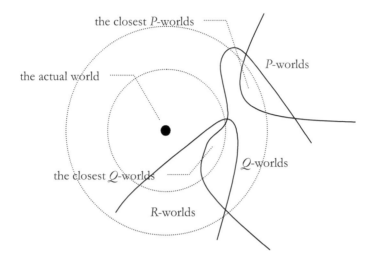

An illustration of the failure of the transitivity of counterfactuals. The closest P-worlds are Q-worlds, and the closest Q-worlds are R-worlds, but the closest P-worlds are not R-worlds.

situation is possible thanks to the fact that the conditionals in the series are evaluated in different possible worlds – the first one in the closest P-worlds, and the second in the closest Q-worlds. Although the nearest P-worlds have to be Q-worlds, and the closest Q-worlds must be R-worlds, from this it doesn't follow that the closest P-worlds are R-worlds.

The lack of transitivity of the causal relation was seen as a problem by Lewis. In order to find a solution, he had to move from the simple counterfactual analysis of causation to a more sophisticated one. In the refined counterfactual approach an event x is a cause of an event y, if y is just counterfactually dependent on x, or there is a chain of intermediate events between x and y such that each event in the chain is counterfactually dependent on the previous one. Hence the planting of the bomb is a cause of the survival of the politician after all, even though the latter is not counterfactually dependent on the former, thanks to the existence of the intermediary event of the defusing of the bomb. As it turns out, the proposed amendment not only corrects the transitivity problem, but also takes care of yet another challenge to the counterfactual analysis. This challenge is created by special cases of so-called redundant causation, to which we will turn our attention in the next section.

Redundant causation

Lewis uses the term "redundant causation" to describe cases in which there is more than one actual event which can causally ensure the occurrence of a particular effect. A typical example of such a situation is an execution by a firing squad. Each shot by itself is sufficient for the condemned person's death. Thus the counterfactual dependence of the death on each individual shot is broken. If one soldier hadn't pulled the trigger, the executed man would have still died because of the remaining shots. Lewis calls this particular example of causal redundancy symmetric, and he insists that in that case our intuitions do not offer a clear answer to the question whether individual shots were indeed causes of the death. According to Lewis's counterfactual analysis only the sum (or, more precisely, the disjunction) of all individual shots counts as a cause. But he argues that this should not worry us much, for the intuitive verdict in this case is unclear. Personally I believe that our intuitions clearly prefer the suggestion that individual fires are causes of the death, but I will not press this point. Instead, let us focus on the even more troublesome case of asymmetric redundancy. Consider the following scenario: two children, Suzy and Billy, are playing a game of throwing stones at a bottle. At a certain point both children take aim at the bottle, but Suzy hurls her stone first and shatters the bottle. At that moment Billy gives up on his throw, which has been pre-empted by Suzy. But the crucial point to observe is that there is no counterfactual dependency between the shattering of the bottle and Suzy's throw. If Suzy hadn't sent her stone, Billy would have, and being an excellent shot, he would most certainly have hit the bottle.

The case of pre-emption clearly spells trouble for the simple counterfactual analysis of causation, for Suzy's throw is unquestionably a cause of the shattering in this case. The pre-empted cause (Billy's readiness to throw his stone) did not participate in the creation of the effect. But the refined version of the counterfactual approach can handle this problem, albeit with some effort. As we recall, according to this analysis two events don't have to be directly connected by the relation of counterfactual dependence to be causally linked. It is sufficient for causality to be present if there is a third event which is counterfactually dependent on the cause, and on which in turn the effect is dependent. We can identify such an event in our case as Suzy's stone flying towards its target at any selected moment after Billy has already given up. Unquestionably this event is counterfactually dependent on Suzy's throw, because if she hadn't thrown the stone, it wouldn't have flown a moment later. But it may be also argued that the shattering of the bottle counterfactually depends on the stone being in midflight. Because Billy is no longer ready to send his stone flying, if Suzy's stone miraculously disappeared, the bottle would be saved. This conclusion depends on several assumptions, one of them being that Suzy's throw pre-empts Billy's attempt before the effect can occur. Because of this feature our considered case of pre-emption is classified as early pre-emption.

But a serious objection can be voiced against the claim of the counterfactual dependence between the shattering and the preceding flight of the stone. It may be suggested that the closest possible world in which there is no stone on its path from Suzy's hand to the target is the world in which Suzy doesn't throw it in the first place. It seems natural that this world should be more similar to the actual world than the one in which the stone disappeared miraculously in midflight. But if the closest worlds in which Suzy's stone is not flying towards the bottle are those in which Suzy did not throw it, then it follows that in those worlds Billy should throw his stone and shatter the bottle. Hence the required counterfactual dependency between the shattering of the bottle and the flight of Suzy's stone is eliminated. Lewis's response to this objection is that we are wrong in our snap judgment regarding the relative similarity of the two possible worlds: the miracle-disappearance world, and the world in which Suzy does not throw her stone. If we followed our unaided intuition and selected the latter world as closer to the actual one, we would have to admit that the following counterfactual is true: if there was no stone flying towards the bottle, Suzy would not have thrown it a moment earlier. This counterfactual is peculiar in that it describes a change located in the past of a given counterfactually assumed event. Lewis calls such counterfactuals backtracking, and he considers them to be in some sense inappropriate (he observes that they even sound strange to our ear). That is, in typical situations we don't accept backtracking counterfactuals. Thus we should apply appropriate criteria of relative similarity between possible worlds in order to eliminate backtracking counterfactuals.

This means that we have to take a closer look at the relation of comparative similarity. One sure-fire way to eliminate backtracking counterfactuals would be to insist that the most similar possible worlds in which a particular contrary-to-fact event takes place are such that the entire past of this event is identical with the actual past. According to this criterion, the closest possible world in which Suzy's stone is not on its path heading towards its target is exactly identical with the actual world up to the considered moment of the flight (thus it contains Suzy's throw, among other events), and at this moment the stone vanishes into thin air. But this solution is too radical for Lewis – not because it admits miraculous disappearances of physical bodies, but because it makes all backtracking counterfactuals false by the stipulation to keep the past unchanged. Lewis is no friend of backtracking counterfactuals, but he admits that in some rare cases they may be true – for instance in cases of time travel or backward causation. For that reason he suggests a new and quite intricate way of comparing possible worlds which takes into account two aspects: their match with the actual world with respect to individual facts and with respect to laws. We don't have space here to present Lewis's proposal in detail, but its key element is that sometimes worlds whose laws don't exactly match the actual laws should be considered closer to the actual world than the worlds which differ from it only with respect to individual facts. This happens when the difference in laws is small and restricted, while the difference in individual facts is widespread.

We can illustrate this with the help of the following example: suppose that we want to consider various possible worlds in which the asteroid that actually wiped out the dinosaurs 65 million years ago narrowly missed the Earth. In one such possible world all the laws of physics are the same as in the actual world, and because the asteroid is on a different trajectory at the moment of its approach to our planet, its entire past history has to be different (this follows from the fact that the laws of celestial mechanics are deterministic). Hence this possible world will differ dramatically from the actual world with respect to individual facts. But there is another way of making the asteroid miss its target – we could simply assume that just before the impact the laws of mechanics temporarily ceased to operate in the region close to the Earth, and the asteroid, instead of following its physically determined path, veered sharply and unpredictably to one side. After this miraculous occurrence everything goes back to normal, but the asteroid is already on a different trajectory, which will take it safely past the Earth. According to Lewis's criterion of similarity, the second world containing a numerically small and spatiotemporally limited suspension of the laws of nature is closer to the actual world than the first world with its entirely different history. In the case of Suzy and Billy this means that the closest world in which Suzy's stone is not heading towards the target is a world in which a miracle either wiped out the stone or at least nudged it slightly so that it no longer followed the same path. No adjustment of the past is permitted (including the fact that Billy didn't throw his stone), and therefore the shattering does not occur. The case seems to be closed.

Late pre-emption

However, a small correction of the considered pre-emption counterexample makes it impossible to solve in such a straightforward way. Suppose that both children actually tossed their rocks, but Suzy was a bit faster and her stone reached the bottle first. Billy's stone, on the other hand, while on target, nevertheless came too late and simply flew through the empty space where the bottle had stood just a second earlier. In that scenario Suzy's throw and the shattering of the bottle are not connected by the causal link even according to the refined counterfactual analysis. There is no intermediate event on which the shattering would be counterfactually dependent, because if anything happened to Suzy's stone, the bottle would be hit by Billy's projectile. This case is referred to in the literature as late pre-emption – the backup cause (Billy's throw) is pre-empted only when the effect takes place. Late pre-emption turns out to be a tough nut to crack for the proponents of the counterfactual approach, and to makes matters worse it may be supplemented by other types of counterexamples as well. In yet another troublesome scenario a soldier is given two identical orders simultaneously by his superiors: a major and a sergeant. The soldier obeys, and it may be claimed that intuitively only the major's order counts as a cause, because his rank is higher than the sergeant's (we say that the major's order trumps the sergeant's, and hence this case is known as trumping pre-emption). But again there is no counterfactual dependence of the soldier's action on the major's order – if the major's hadn't given his order, the solder would have followed the sergeant's order and would have done the same thing.

An interesting attempt to deal with the obstinate cases of late and trumping pre-emption is based on a closer examination of the notion of events underlying the counterfactual analysis of causation. As we remember from Chapter 4, one available conception of events is Kim's property attribution theory. One characteristic feature of events in this approach is that they are, metaphysically speaking, very fragile entities. That is, a small and insignificant change in a given event's properties leads to the loss of its identity. If we apply Kim's account of events to the considered cases we may come to the conclusion that the counterfactual dependence between appropriate events exists after all. For instance, if Suzy's hadn't thrown her stone, the bottle would have been shattered by Billy's stone, but it would have been a qualitatively and numerically different shattering, because Billy's projectile came from a different direction and at a slightly later moment. Hence it may be claimed that in the case in which Suzy didn't toss her stone, the actual shattering would not occur (being replaced by a similar but numerically distinct shattering). In the same vein we may try to deal with the trumping pre-emption case, arguing that there would be some small differences between the way the soldier would execute the major's order and the sergeant's order.

But the fragility solution has one big drawback – namely, it leads to a multiplication of unintuitive, spurious causal links. For instance, if during Suzy's throw a small gust of wind came, this gust would count as a cause of the shattering, because without it the stone would have followed a slightly different path and would have hit the bottle in a slightly different manner, creating a numerically distinct event. This argument convinced Lewis that the fragility approach is inadequate, and that a new solution is required. He claimed to have found such a solution in his newest approach to causation, which appeared in print one year before his sudden death. In this solution he replaced the relation of counterfactual dependence between the cause and the effect with the relation of influence. Roughly, an event x influences another event y if small modifications of x are counterfactually connected with small modifications of y. For instance, if we modified Suzy's throw slightly with respect to its timing, strength, angle, spin, etc., the shattering would be modified accordingly. No such link exists between Billy's throw and the shattering, and therefore there is no causation here. But even this latest in the series of improvements of the counterfactual analysis of causation cannot escape criticism. It may be pointed out that there are unquestionable cases of causal links which nevertheless do not display any sort of influence relation. Throwing a switch at a railway fork and directing the traffic onto the dead-end track counts as a cause of a subsequent train crash, but no modification of the way the switching is executed can result in a modification of the crash. It looks like the quest for a perfect theory of causation does not end with Lewis's latest theory and will have to continue for quite a while.

Causal powers and dispositions

Some philosophers are not entirely satisfied with the analyses of causation presented so far. They complain that all the proposed definitions of the causal relation fail to reveal the metaphysical essence of causation. Instead, these definitions merely offer us more or less adequate criteria which can help us identify causal links existing in the world, but they do not further our understanding of the nature of causation. According to some, the real source of causation lies in the fundamental properties of things called powers. Powers, known also as dispositions, are a special category of properties which determine not what an object possessing them is like, but what this object can do in given circumstances. More precisely, a disposition is a property whose essence is characterized by two elements: its stimulus (or trigger) and its manifestation. An object possesses a disposition if it displays an appropriate manifestation when the triggering condition is present. The oft-used example of a disposition is fragility. A precious vase is fragile, because it breaks when handled roughly. The application of force is a stimulus of fragility, whereas the breaking is its manifestation. It has to be stressed that an object does not have to be actually broken in order to be classified as fragile. The possession of a disposition does not imply that its manifestation is present, only that the manifestation *would be* displayed if the stimulus were present. Thus dispositions are essentially modal properties, as they involve possibility rather than actuality.

According to the dispositional account of causation, effects happen as a result of acting powers. This is not to say that effects are simply manifestations of some dispositions, for effects may occur as a result of many powers acting simultaneously or in a quick

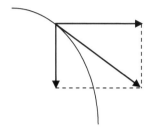

The trajectory of a projectile in a gravitational field. The direction of motion at a given time is determined by the combination of two causal powers: the power of the inertial motion in the horizontal direction, and the power of gravity acting vertically.

succession. As an example let us consider a situation in which a bullet is shot from a gun parallel to the Earth's surface. Ignoring the air resistance we can say that the trajectory of the bullet after leaving the muzzle is a result of the action of two powers: the power of the material body (e.g. the bullet) to move uniformly (i.e. at a constant speed) in the direction in which no force is acting, and the gravitational power of the Earth whose manifestation is the accelerated motion of free objects straight towards the Earth. But the manifestations of these two powers combine together to create a new outcome: a trajectory which has the shape of a parabola. In this particular case the manifestations of the two powers combine according to the well-known rule of adding vectors (the parallelogram rule), but generally these rules may be much more complicated or even non-existent.

Dispositional properties pose several challenges for those philosophers who want to use them as the basis for causation. The first problem that has to be faced is how to distinguish dispositions from non-dispositions (also known as categorical properties). The standard response to this question is given in the form of the conditional analysis of dispositions. According to it, the possession of a dispositional property by an object x is equivalent to the truth of the counterfactual conditional "If x were to undergo stimulus S, x would display manifestation M". But this analysis is open to serious objections. Suppose, for instance, that a live wire is connected to a

CAUSATION

device which cuts off the power the moment anything touches it. If we agreed to define the wire's property of being live as the disposition to deliver an electric shock when touched, then we would have to conclude wrongly that the wire is not live, because the counterfactual conditional "If I touched this wire, I would be electrocuted" is false, given the existence of the safety device. This example illustrates a general situation in which the stimulus eliminates the disposition before its manifestation can occur (such instances are called cases of "finkish dispositions" or "finks" in the literature). Another troublesome scenario is when the process leading from the stimulus to the manifestation is interrupted by an interfering factor called an antidote. It should be clear that taking an antidote does not eliminate the intrinsic power of a poison to kill those who ingest it but only renders it ineffective. Several proposals of how to improve the simple conditional analysis of dispositions have been put forward, but none of them has reached the status of a universally accepted solution.

Another intensely debated problem is the question of the existence of so-called ungrounded powers. Typical examples of dispositions, such as fragility or solubility, are known to be reducible to more fundamental properties. That a substance is fragile or soluble depends on its molecular structure, which is causally responsible for the creation of the manifestation (breaking or dissolving). In such cases dispositions turn out to be grounded in more basic properties (which may or may not happen to be categorical). But does this have to be the case? Can there be dispositions not reducible to anything more fundamental? Some philosophers insist that there is nothing fundamentally wrong with the idea of an ungrounded disposition. Consider for instance an electron. Its electric charge can be interpreted as the disposition to behave in a certain way in an electromagnetic field (for instance to accelerate in the direction of the electric force). But can this disposition be reduced to anything more fundamental? What can be more fundamental than the charge of an electron? According to the standard model, electrons are considered true elementary particles with no internal structures, so there is no lower structural level to which the properties of the electron could be reduced to. And the charge itself does not seem to be amenable to a further analysis in terms of more basic properties of the electron.

But there is a view even more radical than the one which accepts ungrounded dispositions. Some philosophers claim that ultimately there are only dispositional properties. According to this view, which may be called pan-dispositionalism (or dispositional monism) all genuine properties have dispositional essences. This is of course a very controversial claim. It may be pointed out that there are clearly numerous examples of true categorical properties, such as shape or spatial location. The proponents of dispositional monism must find a way of reinterpreting such properties in dispositional terms as powers to do something. Various suggestions of how to do it have been made in the literature. For instance the property of having three vertices possessed by a triangle can be spelled out in terms of the following disposition: if we counted correctly the vertices, the result would be the number three. However, this disposition does not seem to be fundamental, as it involves sentient beings such as ourselves. A marginally better analysis is for instance present in the attempt to define roundness in terms of the disposition to roll downhill when unsupported.

But even if the pan-dispositionalist managed to find a way to "dispositionalize" all seemingly categorical properties, there are more troubles ahead. As we remember, dispositions are defined in terms of the potential exemplification of two new properties: the stimulus property and the manifestation property. If all properties are dispositional, then these new properties must be interpreted in terms of further stimulus- and manifestation properties, and so on. This procedure seems to end in an infinite regress, which is hard to accept because it implies the existence of an infinity of distinct fundamental properties. An alternative to this is circularity: at a certain point of our analysis we may decide to use the very properties we have started with. At first sight this option looks equally unacceptable, because a circular analysis does not seem to be capable of explicating the nature of dispositional properties. And yet it may be claimed that in some cases such a circular analysis can at least fix the numerical identity of individual dispositional properties. Still dispositional monism remains a heroic stance which for now seems to be fighting an uphill battle.

6 DETERMINISM AND FREE WILL

Causation can be seen as a force which makes things happen. Whether this force acts with necessity is a contentious issue, but some philosophers believe that events in our world do not unfold by accident or chance. According to this view, the entire history of the universe is somehow predetermined, so that there is no room for spontaneity or accidentality. This broad metaphysical hypothesis is known under the name of determinism, and those who oppose it call themselves indeterminists. In this chapter we will first attempt to clarify the thesis of determinism, which is a notoriously ambiguous and multifaceted view. Then we will discuss whether the assumption of determinism should change the way we see ourselves as acting agents. Can we meaningfully talk about the freedom of making decisions in a world in which everything is determined? And if some actions are indeed free in such a world, how to distinguish them from those that aren't?

In popular introductions to the subject determinism is often presented as the claim that everything has its cause. According to this stance events happen for a reason – they do not appear out of thin air. However, this interpretation of determinism (which is also referred to as the principle of causation) heavily depends on the adopted notion of a cause. As we have seen in the previous chapter, there is no shortage of competing conceptions of causality, and each conception leads to a different understanding of what the principle of causation says. For instance, if we followed the counterfactual analysis developed in Chapter 5, this principle would state that every event is counterfactually dependent on some other distinct events. This looks like a very weak statement, and it is hard to imagine a world similar to ours in which it would be violated. Even phenomena which according to modern science may deserve to be called indeterministic seem to satisfy this weak principle. For example, contemporary atomic physics assumes that the process of the radioactive decay of an unstable nucleus is indeterministic in that it is impossible to tell exactly when it will occur (we can only calculate the probability that the nucleus will decay within a certain period of time). But clearly there are plenty of events on which this particular decay counterfactually depends, and which therefore count as its causes. One such cause may be simply the event of the creation of the nucleus (if the nucleus had not been created, it would not have decayed). To avoid this unintuitive consequence the proponents of the principle of causation implicitly assume the interpretation of causes as sufficient conditions. Our best scientific theories imply that the conditions preceding the decay are not sufficient for it to occur, because another atom in perfectly the same conditions may not decay now but in a thousand years. Thus probabilistic processes of radioactive decay would be without causes under this approach.

Determinism, predictions, and laws

There is a long tradition in philosophy to associate determinism with predictability. Predicting future events is one of the main goals of science, which unfortunately can rarely be achieved in practice. We are severely limited in our ability to forecast the weather for a couple of weeks in advance, or to predict such catastrophic events as earthquakes and tsunamis. Pierre Simone de Laplace, a French mathematician, physicist and philosopher working at the turn of the 18th and 19th centuries, thought of one way of overcoming these limitations. Laplace is the author of a famous passage in which he characterizes determinism with the help of the following thought experiment. Imagine a powerful intelligence whose computational and perceptual abilities as well as general knowledge are infinitely greater than ours. This intelligent being (known to posterity as Laplace's demon) would have no problems with predicting every single future event (and every past one, for that matter) if he knew precisely the state the world is in at this very moment.

For Laplace this is the essence of determinism: it should be in principle possible to infer the occurrence of every event at some time t on the basis of the complete and accurate knowledge of the state of the world at another time t'. The main tool with the help of which this can be done is of course the laws of nature. Laplace derived his idea of determinism from the successes of Newtonian mechanics in describing and predicting motions of material bodies under the influence of gravitational forces. The laws of Newtonian mechanics have the mathematical form of second-order linear differential equations, and these equations possess unique solutions if only we fix the initial conditions. This means that if we fix the positions and velocities of all bodies in a given system at a certain instant, and if we take into account all gravitational (or any other) forces acting upon these bodies, we can in principle calculate the trajectory of each individual body. Unfortunately the mathematical calculations required for systems of more than just a couple of bodies are so enormously complicated that even the most powerful computers could not accomplish this task. That's why Laplace had to enlist the help of a supernatural demon.

However, there are several problems with the predictive version of determinism as envisaged by Laplace. First of all, it is unclear what exactly the computational capabilities of the demon are supposed to be. If we assume that the demon works like a "normal" computer but with unlimited storage capacities (a so-called universal Turing machine), then there are reasons to believe that certain necessary computations will never be able to be completed in the required time frame. On the other hand, if we intend to equip the demon with truly supernatural capabilities, then nothing can stop us from assuming that he can simply "divinate" every single future event, thus making the thesis of determinism trivially true. Another controversial issue is the assumption that the demon knows every single detail about the current state of the universe. This is a highly idealistic assumption, as all the quantitative information we can get about the world is always given within a margin of experimental error. To avoid such a controversial presupposition, Karl Popper has proposed a more down-to-earth formulation of predictive determinism which calls for the concept of an ideal scientist rather than that of a supernatural demon. For Popper the thesis of determinism is true if such an ideal scientist could in principle predict future events within a certain, fixed in advance margin of experimental error, if he knew the current

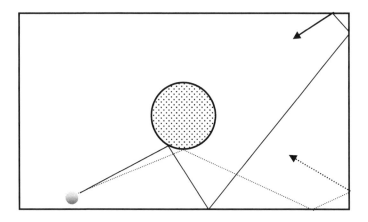

An example of a chaotic but deterministic system. A small variation of
the angle at which the billiard ball is shot snowballs into a huge
difference in trajectory.

state of the system, again with a reasonable degree of precision.
However, it is interesting to observe that there are some systems
which do not satisfy Popper's criterion, even though in a more
fundamental sense they are still deterministic. These are physical
systems which are extremely sensitive to small changes in their initial
conditions, so that even a tiny variation of those conditions results
within a short period of time in a dramatic difference in the evolution
of the system. This phenomenon is aptly called "deterministic
chaos", and it effectively prevents making any reasonable predictions
for such systems, due to the fact that we can never know the initial
conditions precisely enough to calculate their future behavior.

But in a more metaphysical sense chaotic systems of the sort
described above may still be deterministic. The metaphysical idea of
determinism does not invoke any epistemological notions such as
prediction or knowledge. Instead, it focuses entirely on objective
relations between the states of a given system at different instants.
Determinism under this approach is often expressed in the form of
the supposition that the momentary state of a system at one point of
time fixes the states at all subsequent times. But what does it mean
that one state fixes another? One possible interpretation may be that
given the initial state s at time t, for any moment t' later than t there is

exactly one state s' in which the system is at t'. However, this explication cannot be correct. Clearly at any given moment our system (whether it's the entire universe or its part) can be in one state only, thus the thesis of determinism would be trivially true. Perhaps we should add that for any moment t' later than t there is only one *possible* state which the system can be in. Yet even in a perfectly mechanistic system of Newtonian particles with its initial state s it is possible that the system will follow various future evolutions, if we allow for some minor violations of the laws. Thus it should be clear that the thesis of determinism has to mention the laws of nature. A system is deterministic if its momentary state s at a given instant t and the laws under which this system operates logically imply that for any later instant t' the state of the system is no other than s'. To put it more concisely, it is the initial state plus the laws which fix the states at all later moments, in the sense that they eliminate all possible evolutions of the system but one. This type of determinism may be dubbed nomological.

The nomological variant of determinism that we have just arrived at may be alternatively expressed within the framework of possible worlds. We can say that a world w with the set of laws L is deterministic, if any world w' with the same set of laws L which agrees with w with respect to its state at moment t, agrees with w with respect to its states at all later moments. If the laws L happen to be time-reversible, then the above characteristic of determinism also implies that the two worlds w and w' will coincide in the past of the moment t, and that in fact w and w' will be identical. Thus in the time-symmetric case the thesis of determinism can be reduced to the following succinct claim: two distinct worlds with the same set of laws must differ at all moments. The adjective "deterministic" may be applied to worlds or to their laws – we often speak of deterministic laws as opposed to laws of a statistical character, which only describe certain propensities. Deterministic laws, on the other hand, are more restrictive: they admit only one outcome in a particular situation with fixed initial conditions. For the reasons described earlier the laws of classical mechanics are commonly accepted to be deterministic.

However, there is one problem with our formulation of determinism. The problem starts with the question of what exactly the momentary state of a system is. Intuitively, it is a complete description of the system at a given moment: a collection of properties and relations instantiated at this very moment by all objects contained within the system. But it is really crucial that the properties and relations which the state at a moment *t* refers to are indeed possessed by the objects at *t*, and that they do not involve what transpires at moments other than *t*. To explain this requirement, let us consider the situation in which we decided to include into the momentary state *s* of the system at *t* the fact that after five minutes its state will be precisely *s'*. In that case it is trivially true that the state at *t* fixes the state at *t'*, yet this fact has nothing to do with determinism but is a result of our too inclusive characterization of the state at *t*. The requirement we have to impose on momentary states can be expressed shortly by saying that a momentary state has to be intrinsic with respect to the temporal point at which it is taken. No information about other temporal instants can be hidden in it. However, this desideratum creates a serious challenge. The state of a Newtonian mechanical system is typically given by specifying instantaneous positions and velocities of all bodies included in the system. But the instantaneous velocity of a body at a given moment *t* is not exactly intrinsic with respect to this moment. It contains information about the behavior of the body in an infinitely small (so-called "infinitesimal") interval surrounding *t*. If we took a snapshot of our system precisely at the selected moment *t*, we would lose all the information about the movements of the bodies (all bodies would look stationary). Thus it seems that velocities should be excluded from the properties admissible in state descriptions. Unfortunately this move has an unwelcome effect in that it leads to the conclusion that Newtonian mechanics is not deterministic after all. Clearly, the positions of bodies at a given moment do not fix their future positions – we need to know in addition how fast those bodies are moving and in what direction.

However, even if instantaneous velocities are not strictly speaking intrinsic with respect to a given moment, their use in state descriptions does not threaten to make the thesis of determinism trivially true. This is the case, because from the mere fact that at a given moment *t* the velocity of an object equals *v* we can't derive any information about the position and velocity of the object at any moment other than *t*. Fixing the velocity of our body at a given moment constrains its possible trajectories but in a very mild way. Given this constraint, all admissible trajectories plotted on a space-time diagram have to make the same angle with the axis of time at

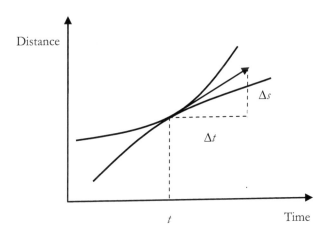

Two different trajectories that have the same instantaneous velocity at
time t. The instantaneous velocity at t is determined by the angle of the
vector tangent to both curves at t (the ratio $\Delta s / \Delta t$).

point t (this angle is precisely the measure of instantaneous velocity,
as it fixes the ratio of distance to time at one moment), but other
than that they can be wildly disparate. Taking that into account, we
can say that velocities are intrinsic "for all practical purposes", and
therefore can be safely admitted into momentary states of systems.
Thanks to this move, Newtonian classical mechanics can be
considered a deterministic theory.

Nomological determinism encounters a serious hindrance in the
form of modern physical theories, especially quantum mechanics.
According to quantum mechanics certain events are not
predetermined by earlier states of the system in question. The most
complete state of a given quantum system plus the laws of quantum
mechanics do not jointly determine the exact results of future
measurements performed on this system but only the probabilities of
obtaining particular values. Thus it is possible to have two identical
systems in precisely the same quantum state such that a measurement
of some parameter (spin, position, energy, etc.) on one particle gives
value a while the result of the same measurement on the other
particle is b. Some physicists and philosophers speculated that there
must be some hidden variables not included in the ordinary quantum
state which can account for this observable difference. If we had a
complete knowledge about the state of the system of interest, we

would be able to predict all results of future measurements. But there are well-known formal results obtainable in quantum mechanics, such as the Bell inequalities or the Kochen-Specker theorem, which place severe restrictions on possible hidden variable theories making them all but impossible. Thus it looks like the full-blown thesis of nomological determinism is no longer a viable metaphysical claim.

Logical determinism and fatalism

The philosophical problem of determinism can be approached from an altogether different angle, independent of the question of nomological relations between separate states of the world. Let us consider a particular future event of which we don't know yet whether it will occur; for instance that on June 30th, 2020, it will be raining in London. We may ask whether it is already "decided" that this is what will happen, or is it still open what the weather will be like on that particular day. One way to spell out this question is in terms of being true *now*: is it true now that it will rain in London or is it not? Note that the question of the truth of the considered sentence is different from the question whether we know that it is true. I don't know how many fish there are in the Pacific Ocean now, but I am sure there is exactly one number n for which the statement "There are n fish in the Pacific Ocean now" is true. But is the case of future contingent statements analogous to this one? Those who believe that statements about future events can be true now (regardless of whether we know them to be true) accept some form of logical determinism. More precisely, logical determinism can be characterized as follows. If a particular event e comes to pass at time t, then for all times t' earlier than t it was true at t' that e would happen at t. Thus if we wait until the end of June in 2020 and see that it is pouring in London, we may confidently say that it was always true that this would happen.

Unfortunately, there is one problem with this version of determinism: it can be easily proven using only an elementary law of logic. The argument dates back to the times of Aristotle, who considered the following example. Imagine that two rival fleets (for instance that of Greece and Persia) are facing each other at sea, each ready to strike at the enemy. But last-minute negotiations are still taking place, so it is not decided yet whether a sea battle will ensue or not. However, regardless of the result of the talks it is already true that either tomorrow there will be a sea battle, or there won't be a sea battle. The simple law of logic on which this statement is based is called the principle of excluded middle, and as the name suggests it states that there is no "middle ground" between the truth of a statement and the truth of its negation. But this means that either it is already true today that the battle will take place, or it is true that there will be no battle. Either way, determinism is vindicated. If the battle really happens, we can say that it always has been the case that there would be a battle (since the other option results in a contradiction), and similarly if the battle is avoided. Hence it looks like everything that actually happens is predestined to happen exactly the way it does, and there is no room for freedom and chance. And all this is guaranteed by logic itself, putting indeterminists in a rather desperate position.

The Polish logician and philosopher Jan Łukasiewicz found this unacceptable. Being an indeterminist himself, he despised the thought that logic could settle such a controversial debate once and for all. In a flash of inspiration, and taking some clues from Aristotle, Łukasiewicz suggested that classical logic needed to be corrected. He cast a critical eye on the law of classical logic known as the principle of bivalence, stating that each statement has one of the two logical values: truth or falsity. This principle seems to be related to the law of excluded middle, but as we will later see is actually an independent law. Łukasiewicz came to the conclusion that indeterminists require a new logical value which is neither truth nor falsity. He variously called it possibility, indeterminacy, or simply the third logical value. If a statement about a future event receives this third value, it means that the event in question has not yet been determined. Łukasiewicz accepted that some future events may be already determined, and therefore statements about them may be already true or false. But the third logical value gives us an opportunity to speak about occurrences not yet decided, such as a future sea battle. Developing his idea further, Łukasiewicz expanded the ordinary method of evaluating complex statements in classical logic, adding new rules of how to handle the third logical value. Thus, for instance, a conjunction of two statements P and Q such that P is true but Q is only possible, is itself possible. But the disjunction "P or Q" of the same statements is true. That way Łukasiewicz obtained a new logic, known as three-valued logic, in which some classical laws are no longer valid. For example the law of excluded middle is not satisfied anymore, because the disjunction of two merely possible statements is itself possible, not true.

Notwithstanding his arguments it may be argued that Łukasiewicz's solution is too radical, and that indeterminism requires no more than a rejection of the principle of bivalence without eliminating any other law of classical logic. Let us look again at the argument proving that in classical logic the thesis of determinism is trivially true. One crucial step of the reasoning is the transition from the instantiation of the principle of the excluded middle "It is true now that there will be a sea battle or there won't be a sea battle" to the statement "Either it is true now that there will be a sea battle, or it is true now that there won't be a sea battle". This step is valid if we assume the principle of bivalence: in a two-valued logic the truth of a disjunction of two statements guarantees that at least one of the statements is true. But this need not be the case if we allow a third logical value. Thus we may insist that the entire disjunction is true now, whereas both disjuncts "There will be a sea battle" and "There won't be a sea battle" are neither true not false (they have the third logical value). There are several ways of incorporating these intuitions into a proper logical calculus. One of them is based on the notion of a supervaluation, which is a valuation of statements with the help of three logical values on the basis of considering first all possible valuations limited to two classical values. The net result of this procedure is that we can have a logic which is entirely classical in all appearances with the exception of the principle of bivalence and some not so important metalogical rules of inference (such as the rule stating that the truth of a disjunction implies the truth of at least one of the disjuncts), and which still leaves room for logical indeterminism.

However, the problem Łukasiewicz wrestled with may be solved in an even simpler way. It may be argued that the entire concept of logical determinism is based on a misunderstanding. The key element of the doctrine of determinism in this approach is the relativization of truth to time. But what is the difference between saying that a given sentence is true at a moment t and saying that it is just true? The phrase "It is true at t that p" suggests that there exists a fact of the matter which occurs at time t and which is directly related to what p reports (while that may be a fact taking place at some later moment t'). But this claim seems to be unfounded. Strictly speaking we know only what it means for a sentence to be true: the sentence "It will rain in London on June 30ᵗʰ 2020" is true, if it will rain in London on that date. Adding to that expression the extra temporal relativization does not change the meaning of the word "true". If we agree with this line of thought, we have to accept that the thesis of logical determinism, far from being a genuine metaphysical claim about reality, is just an empty logical tautology "If it is true that it will rain in London, then it is true that it will rain in London". Łukasiewicz must have been aware of this difficulty, because he made a suggestion that we should interpret the temporally-indexed notion of truth in terms of causality: "It is true at t that an event e will occur" means that at t there exists a cause of its occurrence. But this interpretation reduces logical determinism to the principle of causation, and of course the logical argument in favor of this claim is no longer valid (the logical tautology that either there will be a sea battle of there won't be a sea battle does not imply that at an earlier moment there is a cause of one of the two events). Thus logical determinism turns out to be either vacuous or reducible to an earlier version of determinism.

The confusion surrounding logical determinism is to a certain extent reminiscent of the confusion created by yet another closely related and controversial position known as fatalism. Fatalism is a curious view according to which everything that happens is already predestined, and therefore our actions are futile. Nothing we may do can change our destiny, which is written in the stars. Numerous references to this doctrine can be found in culture and literature, from the famous story of Oedipus in the Greek mythology to Denis Diderot's satire *Jacques le fataliste*. But we will mostly be concerned with the philosophical basis of those myths and stories. How can it be argued that human actions do not change anything in the actual course of events? One type of fatalism can be characterized as religious fatalism. Because God is omniscient, he knows in advance every single event that will unfold in the future, including our actions and their consequences. Thus not only the outcomes of our decisions but even decisions themselves are already fixed and immutable. Logical fatalism, on the other hand, is based on arguments similar to the one considered earlier in the context of logical determinism. The story used in one such argument is set in London during the Blitz in the nineteen forties. An air raid warning is announced and people are seeking refuge in underground bomb shelters. Surprisingly, it may be argued that all precautions that I could implement in this situation are futile, because it is true that either I will be killed in this air raid, or I won't (again we rely on the law of excluded middle). If I am going to die, any precautions I might take will turn out to be ineffective. But if I am to survive this raid, the precautions will be unnecessary. Thus it is not rational to take any precautions whatsoever.

This reasoning strikes us as blatantly (and dangerously) incorrect. However, compare it with the following one. A passenger ship carrying my friend ran aground and sunk in heavy seas yesterday. The list of survivors is still incomplete, so I don't know whether my friend is dead or alive. Does it make sense for me to pray for his survival in this situation? Regardless of whether you generally believe in the power of prayer or not, in this particular case it may be argued that my prayer is pointless. Either my friend is dead or he is alive. If he is dead, my prayer will be ineffective, and if he is alive, my prayer is unnecessary. Why is this case compelling while the earlier argument is not? The answer to this lies in causation. My prayer cannot help, because I am unable to causally influence past events which have already taken place. But in the air raid scenario my survival is a matter of the future, and can still be influenced. The fatal error committed in the Blitz argument is the assumption that if I survive the bombing, my precautions will have been unnecessary. This is incorrect, because I may survive precisely because I have taken precautions. In order to test whether one event is necessary for another, we have to turn to counterfactual reasoning. Suppose I have escaped to the bomb shelter, and during the raid my house has been hit by a bomb. Now we can clearly see that my survival was caused by my decision to take shelter, because if I had stayed home, I would not have survived. But in the shipwreck scenario the analogous counterfactual is false, because it is a backtracking counterfactual. Given that my friend has survived, even if I didn't pray, he would still have survived.

The case for religious fatalism is a bit trickier. Was my decision to run to the shelter irrelevant, because God had possessed the foreknowledge of my survival? If we apply the test of counter-factuality, we may opt for two possibilities. One option is to admit that if I had stayed home, God would have been wrong regarding my survival. This means that we treat the possible world in which the miracle of God's mistake occurs as closest to the actual world. But some would claim that this is incompatible with God's necessary omniscience. In that case we may want to follow the second available option and admit backtracking counterfactuals. If I had decided not to take shelter, God would have had different knowledge beforehand: he would have known that I was going to die. Thus God's knowledge does not preclude the fact that my actions influence my destiny.

Free will

But does it even make sense to speak about free actions in a world which is deterministic? A convincing argument may be given that determinism in the nomological sense precludes the possibility of the existence of free will. The starting point of this argument is the observation that for an action to be genuinely free the acting agent should have several alternatives to choose from. For instance, my decision to go to the movies can be assumed to be free, because before I made up my mind I had had several options: I might have chosen reading about philosophy instead, or going to the park. However, it may be pointed out that if determinism is true, these options are illusory. Given the state of the universe at any particular moment, there is only one future scenario which is compatible with the laws of nature. Let us then select a moment well before I was born. Clearly I cannot influence the state the universe was in a hundred years before my birth. But this state and the laws (which seem to be even more immune from my impact) determine that there is only one possible outcome of my apparent decision: a visit to the cinema. Thus I was no freer in my "decision" than an apple which "freely" falls to the ground as prescribed by the law of gravity. The view according to which free will cannot be reconciled with determinism is known as incompatibilism. In the light of the aforementioned argument it looks like compatibilism is a lost cause. But surprisingly many excellent philosophers, from David Hume to David Lewis, subscribe to this heroic metaphysical stance. What possible arguments can the compatibilists produce which could offset the reasoning from determinism against the freedom of will?

The defenders of compatibilism concentrate their efforts on the notion of free actions, trying to come up with a convincing characterization of freedom which would not collide with determinism. It has to be conceded that freedom of action is a rather equivocal concept which admits many possible interpretations. One natural way to define it is in terms of lack of constraints. We all agree that a person thrown in jail is not free, because his ability to roam around is severely restricted. However, the freedom that the prisoner is lacking is not the freedom in the metaphysical sense that is of interest to us. We all are subject to various constraints: we can't fly or stay alive without oxygen for more than ten minutes. But the essence of metaphysical freedom is that given the actual constraints that are imposed on us, we can still choose freely among the number of options we are left with. To say that a prisoner is free in the metaphysical sense may sound like a cruel joke or at best a crude attempt at consolation, yet it is undeniable that the prisoner can still make choices which we would normally call free. By the same token we have to reject the suggestion that coerced actions are not free in the fundamental sense. I may not be held legally or even morally responsible for following orders given at gunpoint, yet ultimately it is my free decision to comply rather than risk my life which leads to my subsequent actions. If we wanted to look for examples of truly un-free actions, we might think of cases such as being under the influence of mind-controlling devices or mind-altering substances, sleepwalking, or suffering from an obsessive-compulsive disorder.

One may suggest that an action is free when the agent does what she wants. But the agreement between one's desires and one's actions may be accidental. Suppose that I have a device which controls the behavior of a given person, and that at a certain point I use this device to make her scratch her head. But purely by chance, the person under my control wanted to scratch her head quite independently, so the definition is satisfied, and yet the action was not free. We may respond that for an action to be free there should be a causal link between the desire and the action. If we interpret causality in terms of counterfactuals, this requirement will come down to the following criterion: an action is free, if it is the case that the agent would not take it had she not wanted to.

This definition incidentally expresses another intuitive feature commonly held to coincide with the freedom of action, namely the ability to act otherwise. This is how Hume interpreted what it means for us to be freely acting agents. But is this characterization acceptable as it stands? As it turns out there are several problems with it. For starters, a kleptomaniac may truthfully say that he might have refrained from shoplifting if he had wanted to, but sadly it is not possible for him to want otherwise. So perhaps we should add as an extra requirement that it must be possible, in a suitable sense, for the agent to want otherwise.

Even if we accepted the proposed characteristic of free actions, does it confirm the compatibilist's standpoint that freedom can coexist with determinism? At first it may look that indeed this is the case. As we have learned in the previous chapter, counterfactual statements may be true even in deterministic worlds. In order to evaluate the statement "If I had wanted, I would have gone for a walk instead of going to the cinema", we consider the possible world in which a small miracle interrupts the deterministic process leading to my desire to see a movie and instead creates an urge to go for a walk. But this method of evaluating counterfactuals creates a problem. It looks like we have to admit that we are capable of breaking the laws as a result of our actions – if I had gone for a walk, some laws would have been violated. Lewis tries to repel this objection by making a distinction between doing something that breaks the law, and causing the laws to be broken. He argues that compatibilism implies only the possibility of the former, not the latter occurrence. More specifically, he claims that while it is true that if I had gone for a walk instead of seeing a movie, some law would be violated, it is not true that one particular law would be violated, because there is more than one way of making me deviate from my deterministically fixed path. Perhaps Lewis is right on that, but being able to do something which breaks some law seems in itself quite worrisome. And, besides, is the capability of doing otherwise really sufficient for a free action to take place? Under Lewis's interpretation of counterfactual sentences, even the apple falling on the ground is capable of "doing otherwise", since there is a possible world in which the law of gravity temporarily ceases to operate, and the apple flies away unimpeded. But this does not prove that the apple possesses free will on its own.

Moreover, it may be argued that the existence of alternative possibilities interpreted counterfactually is not a necessary condition for the freedom of action either. John Locke used the following example to illustrate this fact: suppose that I sit in a room with its door shut, not knowing that the door is in fact locked. I decide to stay in the room, and my decision seems to be free. But in reality I didn't have any choice: if I had decided to leave the room, I would not have been able to open the door. Harry Frankfurt, a contemporary moral philosopher, gave another example pointing in the same direction. Imagine that Larry pushes Freddy of his own will, but unbeknownst to Larry, George is monitoring his mental state, and if Larry showed any sign of hesitation, George would use a mind-controlling device to make him push Freddy anyway. Thus Larry doesn't have any alternative (even if he didn't want to push Freddy, he would still do it), and yet his action is free. It is worth noting that this example is a clear case of pre-emption similar to the ones considered in Chapter 5, in which there is a causal link between Larry's desire to push Freddy and his action, in spite of the fact that no counterfactual dependence exists between the two events (because of the pre-empted backup cause in the form of George and his mind-controlling machine). This fact suggests a defense strategy similar to the one used in the original case of pre-emption. We may insist that Larry's desire is a cause of his action after all, because there is a moment between his decision and the act of pushing at which George gives up on pressing the button of his device, and therefore there is a chain of counterfactually dependent events leading from the cause to the effect. Thus it may still be claimed that an action is free if the desire to perform it is its cause, even though the counterfactual dependence may not be present. Causality, and not the existence of counterfactually interpreted alternatives, may be the key to free will after all.

FURTHER READING

Introduction

There are plenty of excellent books on the subject of contemporary metaphysics available on the market, ranging from elementary introductions to more advanced surveys. Brian Garrett, *What Is This Thing Called Metaphysics?* (Routledge, 2006) is a very accessible introductory book aimed at absolute beginners. Slightly more demanding textbooks are Michael J. Loux, *Metaphysics: A Contemporary Introduction* (3th edition, Routledge, 2006) and E.J. Lowe, *A Survey of Metaphysics* (Oxford University Press, 2002). Stephen Lawrence, Cynthia Macdonald (eds.), *Contemporary Readings in the Foundations of Metaphysics* (Blackwell, 1998) is a collection of important papers in various areas of metaphysics, with state-of-the-art introductions to each section commissioned from prominent philosophers especially for this volume. Another useful collection is Steven D. Hales, *Metaphysics: Contemporary Readings* (Wadsworth, 1999). The most authoritative compendium on recent metaphysics is Michael J. Loux, Dean W. Zimmerman (eds.) *The Oxford Handbook of Metaphysics* (Oxford University Press, 2003), but this source is not recommended for first-time learners.

Chapter 1

Modern reconstructions of Alexius Meinong's theory of nonexistent objects can be found in Terence Parsons, *Nonexistent Objects* (Yale University Press, 1980) and Colin McGinn, *Logical Properties* (Clarendon, 2000), especially chapter "Existence". Peter van Inwagen, "McGinn on existence", *The Philosophical Quarterly* 2008 (58), pp. 36-58 contains an in-depth criticism of contemporary versions of Meinongianism. The classic solution of the problem of negative existentials, which paved the way to the quantifier view of existence, is presented in Bertrand Russell, "On denoting", *Mind* 1905 (14), pp. 479-493, reprinted in Bertrand Russell, *Essays in Analysis* (Allen and Unwin, 1973), pp. 103-119. Another cornerstone paper on the quantifier view and the problem of ontological commitment is Willard v. O. Quine, "On what there is" in W. v. O. Quine, *From a Logical Point of View* (Harper and Row, 1963), pp. 1-19, reprinted in Stephen Lawrence, Cynthia Macdonald (eds.), *Contemporary Readings in the Foundations of Metaphysics* (Blackwell, 1998), pp. 32-45. A rigorous but still readable introduction to the philosophical and logical analysis of identity is John Hawthorne, "Identity", in Michael J. Loux, Dean W. Zimmerman (eds.) *The Oxford Handbook of Metaphysics* (Oxford University Press, 2003), pp. 99-130. The classical text presenting a critical discussion of the Principle of the Identity of Indiscernibles is Max Black, "The identity of indiscernibles", *Mind* 1952 (LXI), pp. 153-164, reprinted in Jaegwon Kim, Ernest Sosa (eds.), *Metaphysics: An Anthology* (Blackwell 1999), pp. 66-71. Katherine Hawley "Identity and indiscernibility", *Mind* 2009 (118), pp. 101-119 is a very well written survey of various possible responses to the counterexamples to PII. The problem of identity and indiscernibility in the context of modern physics (especially quantum mechanics) is extensively analysed in Steven French and Decio Krause, *Identity in Physics: A Formal, Historical and Philosophical Approach* (Oxford University Press, 2006). The proposal to replace absolute discernibility with weak discernibility in the case of quantum particles is discussed in Simon Saunders, "Are quantum particles objects?", *Analysis* 2006 (66), pp. 52-63.

Chapter 2

David M. Armstrong, *Universals: An Opinionated Introduction* (Westview Press, 1989) is a recommended first reading about the problem of universals. A very well-written overview of the epistemology and ontology of universals can be found in Bertrand Russell, *Problems of Philosophy* (Clarendon Press, 1912, available on-line), chapters IX and X. Those interested in the technical details of metalinguistic nominalism may consult the rather difficult piece by Willfried Sellars, "Abstract entities", *Review of Metaphysics* 1963. Gonzalo Rodriguez-Pereyra "Resemblance nominalism and the imperfect community", *Philosophy and Phenomenological Research* 1999 (59), pp. 965-982 contains a discussion of the main problems of resemblance nominalism with some suggested solutions. Keith Campbell, *Abstract Particulars* (Blackwell, 1990) is a monograph devoted to trope theory. Bob Hale, *Abstract Objects* (Blackwell, 1987) develops an account of abstract objects whose starting point is Frege's abstraction principle. A thorough and quite accessible survey of various nominalistic interpretations of mathematics is John P. Burgess and Gideon Rosen, *A Subject with No Object: Strategies for Nominalistic Interpretations of Mathematics* (Clarendon Press, 1997). Geoffrey Hellman, *Mathematics without Numbers* (Clarendon Press, 1989) develops a modal interpretation of mathematical theories, but it is appropriate only for readers with considerable expertise in mathematics and formal logic. The Indispensability Argument for the existence of mathematical objects, also known as the Quine-Putnam argument, can be found in Hilary Putnam, *Philosophy of Logic* (George Allen & Unwin, 1971). A fictionalist response to the Indispensability Argument is the topic of the provocative book by Hartry Field, *Science without Numbers* (Blackwell, 1980). The problem caused by multiple reductions of numbers to set theory was noted and discussed by Paul Benacerraf in his "What numbers could not be", *Philosophical Review* 1965 (74), reprinted in Paul Benacerraf and Hilary Putnam, *Philosophy of Mathematics: Selected Readings* (Cambridge University Press, 1982), pp. 272-294. The structuralist interpretation of mathematics is developed in Michael Resnik, *Mathematics as a Science of Patterns* (Clarendon Press, 1997). A recent discussion of the bundle theory can be found in James Van Cleve, "Three versions of the bundle theory", *Philosophical Studies* 1985 (47), pp. 95-107, reprinted in Stephen Lawrence, Cynthia Macdonald (eds.), *Contemporary Readings in the Foundations of Metaphysics*

(Blackwell, 1998), pp. 264-274. The nuclear theory of particulars is developed by Peter Simons in "Particulars in particular clothing: three trope theories of substance", *Philosophy and Phenomenological Research* 1994 (54), pp. 553-575, reprinted in Stephen Lawrence, Cynthia Macdonald (eds.), *Contemporary Readings in the Foundations of Metaphysics* (Blackwell, 1998), pp. 363-384.

Chapter 3

An accessible introduction to modal notions and possible worlds is Theodore Sider, "Reductive theories of modality", in Michael J. Loux, Dean W. Zimmerman (eds.) *The Oxford Handbook of Metaphysics* (Oxford University Press, 2003), pp. 180-208. David Lewis's controversial account of possible worlds was first sketched in his chapter "Possible worlds" of the book *Counterfactuals* (Harvard University Press, 1973), reprinted in Stephen Lawrence, Cynthia Macdonald (eds.), *Contemporary Readings in the Foundations of Metaphysics* (Blackwell, 1998), pp. 96-101, and was further developed in *On the Plurality of Worlds* (Blackwell, 1986). Alvin Plantinga's actualism is presented in his "Actualism and possible worlds", *Theoria* 1976 (42), pp 139-160. Saul Kripke's argument for the necessity of identity is given in his "Identity and necessity" in M.K. Munitz (ed.), *Identity and Individuation* (New York University Press, 1971), pp. 135-164, reprinted in Jaegwon Kim, Ernest Sosa (eds.), *Metaphysics: An Anthology* (Blackwell 1999), pp. 72-89.

Chapter 4

The literature on the philosophical topic of time is enormous, and no list of readings of a reasonable length can even come close to being complete. For absolute novices in this area I recommend as an introduction the engaging and easy-to-read book by Robin Le Poidevin, *Travels in Four Dimensions. The Enigmas of Space and Time* (Oxford University Press, 2003). The linguistic argument in favor of the existence of events is given in Donald Davidson, "The logical form of action sentences", in Nicholas Rescher (ed.), *The Logic of Decision and Action* (University of Pittsburgh Press, 1967), pp. 81-95. Davidson's conception of events can be found in his "The individuation of events" in Nicholas Rescher (ed.), *Essays in Honor of Carl G. Hempel* (Reidel, 1969), reprinted in Stephen Lawrence,

Cynthia Macdonald (eds.), *Contemporary Readings in the Foundations of Metaphysics* (Blackwell, 1998), pp. 295-309. Jaegwon Kim "Events as property exemplifications", in M. Brand, D. Walton (eds.), *Action Theory* (Reidel, 1976), pp. 159-177, reprinted in Stephen Lawrence, Cynthia Macdonald (eds.), *Contemporary Readings in the Foundations of Metaphysics* (Blackwell, 1998), pp. 310-325 presents an alternative theory of events and their identity conditions. The distinction between the A-series and the B-series is introduced in John McTaggart, *The Nature of Existence*, vol. 2 (Cambridge University Press, 1927), chapter XXXIII. J.E. Lowe's critique of McTaggart's proof of the unreality of time, which we mentioned in the chapter is laid out in *A Survey of Metaphysics* (Oxford University Press, 2002), pp. 316-319. Another important commentary on McTaggart's seminal argument is Michael Dummett, "A defense of McTaggart's proof of the unreality of time", *Philosophical Review* 1960 (69), pp. 497-504. Donald C. Wiliams, "The myth of passage", *Journal of Philosophy* 1951 (48), pp. 457-472, and J.J.C. Smart, *Philosophy of Scientific Realism* (Routledge, 1963), Chapter VII "The space-time world", contain clear expositions of the B-theory of time. Tim Maudlin's response to the "second per second" objection against the idea of the flow of time can be found in his *The Metaphysics within Physics* (Oxford University Press, 2007), Chapter 7 "On the Passing of Time". Peter Forrest, "Relativity, the passage of time and the cosmic clock" in Dennis Dieks (ed.) *Ontology of spacetime II* (Elsevier, 2008), pp. 245-253 contains an attempt to rehabilitate the passage of time in modern cosmology. Arthur Prior's challenge to the B-theory is formulated in his "Thank goodness that's over", *Philosophy* 1959 (34). The recent book Craig Bourne, *A Future for Presentism* (Oxford University Press, 2006) is an extended defense of the presentist theory of time. Sidney Shoemaker's argument for the possibility of time without change is developed in his "Time without change" in R. Le Poidevin, M. MacBeath (eds.) *The Philosophy of Time* (Oxford University Press, 1993). Nick Huggett and Carl Hoefer, "Absolute and Relational Theories of Space and Motion" in Edward N. Zalta (ed.), *The Stanford Encyclopedia of Philosophy (Fall 2009 Edition)*, , URL = http://plato.stanford.edu/archives/fall2009/entries/spacetime-theories/ is an excellent survey of the debate on the nature of space and time from Newton and Leibniz to Einstein. Tim Maudlin makes the distinction between the static shift argument and the kinematic shift argument in his "Buckets of water and waves of space: why space-time is probably a substance", *Philosophy of Science* 1993 (60), pp. 183-203. The problems of the thermodynamic arrow of time are nicely exposed in David Albert, *Time and Chance* (Harvard University Press, 2000), and on a more advanced level in Lawrence Sklar, *Physics and Chance* (Cambridge University Press, 1993), chapter 10 "The direction of time". The thesis that time travel is fundamentally possible is defended in David Lewis, "The paradoxes of time travel", *American Philosophical Quarterly* 1976, pp. 145-152, reprinted in David Lewis, *Philosophical Papers Vol. II* (Oxford University Press, 1986), pp. 67-74. Katherine Hawley, *How Things Persist* (Oxford University Press, 2001) is a monograph devoted to the problem of existing in time. The argument from amputation is developed and analyzed in Peter van Inwagen, "The doctrine of arbitrary undetached parts", *Pacific Philosophical Quarterly* 1981 (62), pp. 123-137, and Mark Heller, "Temporal parts of four-dimensional objects", *Philosophical Studies* 1984 (46), pp. 323-334, reprinted in Steven D. Hales, *Metaphysics: Contemporary Readings* (Wadsworth, 1999), pp. 468-475. The notion of identity relativized to kinds, which is not transitive, is developed in P.T. Geach, "Identity", *Review of Metaphysics* 1967 (21), pp. 2-12.

Chapter 5

D.H. Mellor, *The Facts of Causation* (Routledge, 1995) defends facts as arguments of the causal relation. The two sides of the debate on whether negative causation should be admitted can be compared in Phil Dowe and Jonathan Schaffer, "Are causes physically connected to their effects?", in Christopher Hitchcock, *Contemporary Debates in Philosophy of Science* (Blackwell, 2004), pp. 187-216. A clear exposition of the nomological conception of causality is given in Rudolf Carnap, *An Introduction to the Philosophy of Science*, (Dover, 1995), pp. 187-196. John Mackie, *The Cement of the Universe* (Oxford University Press, 1974) contains an account of his own INUS conception. The counterfactual conception of causation found its first formulation in David Lewis, "Causation", *Journal of Philosophy* 1973 (70), pp. 556-567, reprinted in Jaegwon Kim, Ernest Sosa (eds.), *Metaphysics: An Anthology* (Blackwell, 1999), pp. 436-443. A necessary background reading for everybody who is serious about the counterfactual approach is David Lewis, *Counterfactuals* (Harvard University Press, 1973). J. Collins, N. Hall, and L. A. Paul (eds.), *Causation and counterfactuals* (Cambridge University Press, 2004) is a comprehensive collection of recent papers on the subject of counterfactual causality. Lewis's latest influence theory of causation is criticized in Tomasz Bigaj, "Causation without influence", *Erkenntnis* 2012 (76), pp. 1-22. The metaphysics of dispositional properties is thoroughly discussed in the following monographs: Stephen Mumford, *Dispositions* (Oxford University Press, 1998), George Molnar, *Powers. A Study in Metaphysics* (Oxford University Press 2003), Alexander Bird, *Nature's Metaphysics: Laws and Properties* (Clarendon Press, 2007).

Chapter 6

John Earman, *A Primer on Determinism* (Reidel, 1986) is a rather advanced (in spite of the title) analysis of different variants of determinism done mostly in the context of physics, but Chapter II "Defining Determinism" should be accessible to beginners. Karl Popper's account of scientific determinism can be found in his *The Open Universe* (Rowman and Littlefield, 1982). The question of the nature of instantaneous velocities and its impact on the issue of determinism is thoroughly analyzed in Frank Arntzenius, "Are there really instantaneous velocities?", *The Monist* 2000 (83), pp. 187-208, and Sheldon R. Smith, "Are instantaneous velocities real and really instantaneous?", *Studies in History and Philosophy of Modern Physics* 2003 (34), pp. 261-280. Logical determinism and its connection with three-valued logic is discussed in Jan Łukasiewicz, "On the notion of possibility", "On three-valued logic", "On determinism", in Storrs McCall, *Polish Logic 1920-1939* (Oxford University Press, 1967), pp. 15-39. David Lewis discusses his variant of compatibilism in "Are we free to break the laws?", *Theoria* 1981 (47), pp. 113-121. A nice, accessible but rigorous exposition of main arguments in the debate on the compatibility of free will with determinism is Ted Warfield, "Compatibilism and incompatibilism: some arguments", in Michael J. Loux, Dean W. Zimmerman (eds.) *The Oxford Handbook of Metaphysics* (Oxford University Press, 2003), pp. 613-630.

INDEX

INDEX

INDEX

numerical, 13–15
qualitative, 13
Identity of Indiscernibles, Principle
of, 15–19, 41, 80
in trope theory, 29
impenetrability assumption, 92
incompatibilism, 130
indiscernibility. *See* identity,
qualitative
Indispensability Argument, 33
indistinguishability postulate in
quantum mechanics, 18
instantaneous velocities, 123
INUS condition, 101–2

K

Kant, Immanuel, 2
Kim, Jaegwon, 62
kinematic shift, 80
Kripke, Saul, 55–58

L

laws of nature, 100
Leibniz, Gottfried, 2, 80–81
Leibniz's law, 15
Lewis, David, 50–53, 87, 96, 104–
14, 130, 132
linearity, 64
Locke, John, 42, 132
logical positivism, 2
logical values, 31
low entropy hypothesis, 86
Lowe, Jonathan, 72
Łukasiewicz, Jan, 126–28

M

Mach, Ernest, 81–82

Mackie, John, 101–4
mathematical objects, 31–35
Maudlin, Tim, 74, 80
McTaggart, John, 69–73
Meinong, Alexius, 6
mereological composition, 36
method of paraphrase, 12, 26, 32
modal realism, 50–53
momentary state, 122
moments, 64

N

necessary condition, 101, 103
necessity, 47–48
Newton, Isaac, 80–82
Newton's bucket experiment, 81–
82
nominalism, 25–28
austere, 26
metalinguistic, 27
resemblance, 28
with respect to mathematical
objects, 32–34
non-existent objects, 6–9

O

ontic categories, 2
ontological commitment, 12, 31
ontological proof, 9
ontology, 1

P

pan-dispositionalism. *See*
dispositional monism
particulars, 20
reductive theories of, 39–44
the bundle theory of, 39–41

This book can be ordered at
https://www.createspace.com/3714583

ABOUT THE AUTHOR

Tomasz Bigaj is a lecturer at the Institute of Philosophy, University of Warsaw, Poland. He has been a Fulbright fellow at the University of Michigan, Ann Arbor, and a Marie Curie fellow at the University of Bristol, UK. His main areas of specialization are philosophy of science (especially of physics), metaphysics, and philosophical logic. He is the author of three books and over thirty professional articles published in peer-reviewed journals (including *Journal of Philosophical Logic*, *Synthese*, *Erkenntnis*, *Philosophy of Science*, *Metaphysica*). His latest book is *Non-locality and Possible Worlds: A Counterfactual Perspective on Quantum Entanglement* (Ontos Verlag, 2006).